LIVING WELL

Making a Difference

Andy Andersen 11/30/12

Mark Anderson,
thanx for all
you do! Andy Anden

Reserved for your special message

To my wife, Cindy, who gets this message better than I, and whose loving support proves that I am truly doing better than I deserve.

Special Thanks To:

Matt and Brad, two fine gentlemen who continue to make dad very proud.

My mom and dad, for their love and for providing the foundation for my life.

My sister Deanna, and brothers Billy, John, and "Jimmy Sopher," for adding so much joy to my childhood.

Commodore Dick Norwood, Admirals Scott Semko and Phil Coady. For your inspiration and leadership throughout my naval career.

Phil Callaway, for his book, *Making Life Rich Without Any Money,* and for whose continuing inspiration has provided the catalyst to both my oral and written message.

My pastor, Kevin Pound, for his guidance in deepening my faith, and whose wonderful oratory skills have sharpened my sword.

Jeff Bryan and Cari Boyce for pushing me over the edge and giving me the knowledge and fortitude to go forth and make this dream a reality.

America—I am honored and humbled to have walked the earth on your soil, and pray this book makes a difference to your wonderful inhabitants and maybe those beyond your shores.

Dusty, my four-legged best friend, who taught me the meaning of unconditional love.

Table of Contents

Preface

Thank you for taking time to read this book. I hope the thoughts and ideas shared here help convey the passion in my heart for improving lives. I believe that making a difference in the lives of those we touch improves our world, thereby making us feel better about ourselves, which is the true essence of living well. Life is too short to approach it any other way.

I may be one of a handful of writers who started their speaking career before writing a book. As I sit on this Southwest flight somewhere between Nashville, Tennessee and Jacksonville, Florida, I find myself reflecting on the events that brought me to this point.

In the cockpit of this 737 sits a former junior officer and pilot of the first Navy squadron I commanded. His name is Kirk "Lucy" Simonian. He attended one of my motivational seminars in Atlanta last year. He just said to me before I boarded this plane, "Skipper, you need to market yourself. America needs to hear your message. It's time to write a book."

So, I'm writing this book for people like "Lucy" who continue to help me fly in the right direction—to nudge me forward—and for you, my readers, who chose to spend hard-earned money and time on my message.

My goal is to leave you feeling better about yourself, your neighbor, and your country. America is a wonderful country, yet many who live here are unhappy—perhaps more so than ever before. As a matter of fact, one study I read indicated that 30 percent of women in this country are depressed, while men are suffering from depression at approximately half that rate, but are gaining quickly. In fact, the fastest growing segment of the population taking anti-depressant drugs is preschoolers! Where are we headed as a society?[1]

We have more wealth, more time saving devices, and more stuff in general. Still, many of us walk around simply existing, wasting the few heartbeats that remain. Then before we know it, we're in a hospice bed ready to pass on to the next world, having spent most of our time focused on the wrong *things* while we were in this world.

America is in desperate need of healing, a kind word, and a smile—something to just make people feel better. The pace and noise of society is making us lose sight of the basic principle upon which America was founded: an abiding concern for family and neighbors, the kind of care and concern that produces a synergy of community and human bonding. That's why we're on this earth. We're surrounded by terrorist attacks, failing economies, college massacres, eroding families, road rage, and television shows that promote ratings but not the values and principles that lead to true happiness and joy.

The substance of my message and the current title of my motivational presentation is "Living Well by

Preface

Making a Difference." The central theme of my presentation is altruistic egoism, which may seem like a contradiction in terms when, in reality, it is a truism. In other words, you end up feeling better about yourself by caring more about others. In fact, John Tesh mentioned on his radio show that our brain actually releases chemicals that physically make us feel better when we do something good for someone else. You see, when we are wrapped up in ourselves, we make a pretty small package.

The purpose of this book is to describe several ideas and techniques to help us achieve this state of altruistic egoism. It's not rocket science. I am amazed at how this message keeps gaining momentum though it's so basic and simple.

I want you to know, as you read my words and feel my passion, that I have not had a perfect life.

I was mugged when I was six years old in my south side Chicago, mobile home neighborhood. My parents argued quite a bit during my childhood (period of adjustment...but still married after fifty-five years...God bless 'em). I ended up giving up my dream to be a doctor when Dad said he did not have the means to help me, hence my naval career. My wife and first son both almost died during his delivery. My marriage has been good, but living with the same person for thirty-two years is not easy and takes work, as I'll discuss. I too struggle with the concepts presented here. I am an average human being with my share of sins, weaknesses, and faults, but I do the best I can with whatever I have.

These days, my wife, Cindy, and I are doing well. I have two wonderful sons, who make me very proud because they get what I'm about to share with you, even though I wasn't always a model father...or husband. I wish I could have some of those moments back, but after fifty-four years of walking this earth, I've learned much and want to share my thoughts and insights into the crazy time we spend on this tiny speck in the immense universe.

Many of my audiences are retiring and active duty Navy/Marine Corps personnel all over the United States. To these audiences, I present financial and motivational seminars. The two comments I hear most often following these seminars are, "Why didn't I hear this message at the beginning of my career?" and "Would you please write a book so I can take your message with me and reference it as my life unfolds."

As a former Navy pilot, I, like the men and women in my military audiences, am fond of quick, hard-hitting checklists that I can refer to in order to stay alive and out of trouble.

My plan is to make this a short, easy read book as well as one that can be used as kind of a reference manual. As such, I have included a checklist at the end of each chapter, beginning with Chapter II, to help you reflect on what you have learned and focus on those things that will make life better for you and those around you in the short time we have together in this world.

The checklists are intended to help you focus on areas of your life that may need work. They are for you to fill out. I recommend using a pencil so you can update the checklist for areas you have improved or fixed as your life evolves. You may want to keep your checklist book in your sock drawer. In this way, you can track your progress toward becoming a better you! After all, we're all under construction until the day we die.

I want this book to serve the same purpose as cockpit checklists and help you through this crazy flight called life, because it's pretty short, and we want to make the most of it. We are all just a wisp in time. So let's make it count by making a difference.

Sit back and let's think about life together.

Chapter I
Evolution

This "making a difference" concept was born out of necessity in 1993 when, as executive officer of Patrol Squadron Sixteen in Puerto Rico, I was approached by a young Navy petty officer with $500 to invest. He had heard I knew something about investing. I asked a few financial questions and soon found myself surrounded by inquisitive sailors. It was obvious to me that they needed guidance in a critical area of sailor's development, which was largely being ignored. I put together a lecture on financial basics that also focused on developing a positive attitude and living within your means, as debt is usually caused by a focus on materialism and a "keeping up with the Joneses" mentality.

(In addition, statistics show that financial issues are the number one cause of domestic disputes and divorce, not infidelity as some might assume. Financial concerns can also lead to problems in the workplace.)

My lecture became popular, and before long, I was training multiple squadrons in Jacksonville, Florida. I even was called upon to testify in front of a United States Senate Subcommittee about how poor finances directly impact military readiness. I also was honored to appear live on C-Span to speak during the launch of the Navy's Personal Financial Management Program at the Pentagon, at the request of the secretary of the Navy's office.

Andy speaking to Pentagon media with
Chief Petty Officer Nolan, 2000

Through it all, I struggled with a fear of public speaking. For those of you who don't know, public speaking is one of the top fears in the world—more frightening than death. Most people would prefer to be in the casket than delivering the eulogy.

In 1994, I continued to face that number one fear in a big way. I had to give a Navy change of command speech to an audience of roughly six hundred sailors and friends. I was scared to death. I had been dreading that moment since the day I knew I was going to command a Navy squadron. When the time came to give my speech, my knees were knocking.

My guest speaker was CBS-golf color analyst and longtime family friend, Ken Venturi. Ken was accustomed to public speaking and television appearances. I, on the other hand, was a basket case.

I had decided that my subject was not going to be military readiness, world threats, or terrorism because, as members of the military, we are inundated with those subjects, more so than civilians are. In addition, those subjects often lose the crowd, and I felt my audience could use a break. So I focused on people and hearts, and what I called the trifecta—faith, families, and friends.

As I spoke, something peculiar happened. My voice quivered at first and I stumbled through the speech I had prepared, but I was amazed to see that my audience actually seemed to be listening to what I had to say…and enjoying it. They were laughing and a few tears even hit the hangar deck. I began to relax and realized that people not only need help, they want help.

They need to hear something that will help them find peace and quality in life, not intensify their already overstressed situations. I soon grew very comfortable with an audience and embraced any opportunity to have a positive impact on the lives of others, even if it meant a lifetime of public speaking.

The next phase of this evolution took place in Washington DC in 1998 at the center of US military headquarters—the Pentagon. I was quite busy as a Navy commander, but as you can imagine, working at the Pentagon was very interesting.

I worked as one of several military assistants for the Secretary of Defense from 1996 to 1999.

The Secretary of Defense, appointed by President Clinton, was Senator Bill Cohen. Mr. Cohen was a fine gentleman who truly cared about his job and the troops his decisions directly affected. I can remember seeing him struggle with important decisions, wondering not only what the impact would be on America, but also on all the military men and women who served this great country and their families. He had a good heart and I considered it an honor to work for him. His wife, Janet Langhart Cohen, also was a gem, and wonderful with the troops. She was a terrific person and she and Secretary Cohen complimented one another well.

There were about ten military assistants working for Secretary Cohen. The two senior aides were two of the finest leaders I have ever known—Marine Corps

Evolution

Generals Jim Jones and Jim Mattis. We routinely handled
paperwork and staff issues for Secretary Cohen's review
or signature, and occasionally served as a personal aide
on international and domestic trips. I accompanied
Mr. Cohen in his travels to China, Australia, Malaysia,
and Korea among other destinations.

(I could fill these pages with tales from those travels,
but that's not the focus of this book. This book is not
about me. It's about you...it's about warming your heart
and making your life better.)

Each assistant was given different responsibilities
and accounts or departments that fell under the jurisdic-
tion of, or interacted with, the Department of Defense
(DOD).

My accounts were the White House, the Office of
the Vice President, the Joint Chiefs of Staff, the Navy
(of course, since I was a Navy guy), and the DOD
Comptroller and Public Affairs.

During my tenure with Secretary Cohen, I worked
with two, soon-to-be in the news, members of the DOD
Public Affairs Department, Monica Lewinsky and Linda
Tripp. Little did I know what was transpiring as I dealt
with them on DOD staffing and paperwork issues. As
that scandal, fraught with power struggles, lust, and politics, unfolded, I found myself taking a hard look at life
and what it was all about.

Soon after that scandal broke, I found myself sitting
in Burke United Methodist Church. It was a Sunday

morning service in April of 1998. The pastor, Ed Pruitt, mentioned that he needed some outgoing and caring men to undergo six months of training to become Stephen Ministers and help other men through the rough times in their lives. I can still feel my wife, Cindy's, elbow gouging my side as she said, "That's you."

You see, I'm an off-the-charts extrovert, as you will discover through the pages of this book, and I care very much for my fellow man. It breaks my heart to see people homeless, hungry, or suffering any injustice. But me? How could I be any kind of minister? You must be kidding. I'm a beer drinking naval aviator and, as many will attest, I'm usually the first guy with a lampshade on his head at a party.

Well, that night I decided to do something outside of my nightly routine. I prayed before I went to bed. I asked God to give me some kind of sign if he wanted me to do this in His name. I wasn't even sure this Christian thing that happened two thousand years ago had any truth to it.

That very night, I had a dream. I had never had a religious dream before and I have not had one since, but that night I had a very vivid dream. I was in a large cave that had a cross in it, and hanging on that cross was a man. I could see the blood and sweat on his crown of thorns and could see he had suffered much. I walked to the base of the cross and saw it was Jesus Christ, but he was already dead.

Evolution

Typical Andy Andersen luck—a day late and a dollar short. I could have spoken to Jesus. Then suddenly, He opened His eyes. His hand came off the nail. He reached down to me and said, "I want you to know, I am God, I love you, and I did this for you."

I woke from that dream with an unbelievable feeling that He had come to me and given me my answer. I usually have strange dreams that make no sense and include a cast of goofy characters, but this one was remarkably different. My life would never be the same; I knew I had a mission to help as many people as I could, and leave this world a better place than I found it.

That same year, I was browsing in the Pentagon bookstore when I came upon a book titled, *Making Life Rich Without Any Money* by Phil Callaway. I purchased that book and read it en route to my high school reunion in Midlothian, Illinois. Callaway's message was about learning to focus on the right things in life and learning that happiness does not rely on material things. This is contrary to what society teaches.

That dream and Callaway's book formed the foundation for my mission, and fueled the passion I feel to affect the direction and thought processes of as many folks as possible.

Again, this book is not about me. It's about others, and about caring for family, neighbors, co-workers, even other drivers on the road! What a novel idea. Optimize those heartbeats for the goodness of others and, in so doing, make your own life better!

As 1998 was coming to a close, I was honored to be selected for a major aviation command in the Navy—even a blind squirrel occasionally gets an acorn. I was told that I was headed to VP-30 in Jacksonville, Florida, the P-3 training squadron and, supposedly, the largest squadron in the Navy. I knew I had over twelve hundred hearts and minds to possibly influence.

I took command in the fall of 1999, and I noticed that the troops seemed more miserable than ever. They were merely food processors, simply existing with long faces, not caring about shipmates, and just putting in time. I decided at that moment to re-wicker my financial lecture and talk more about life, marriage, kids, money, smiling at people, letting folks merge into traffic, and buying things from kids at lemonade stands. I authored my talk and Lt. Pete Garvin did a wonderful power point brief of my first presentation "Let's Make It a Wonderful Life by Making a Difference."

Instead of spending five minutes with new check-ins, I had them attend this new, two-hour Life Management Seminar, as the Navy now calls it. It had an amazing affect on morale. Within six months, we had turned the squadron's performance around. We went from being 240 flight-training events behind to sixty ahead. It's not a difficult concept—happy people produce more! If your workers' finances are in order and they get along with their spouses and are happy with life in general, then they are assets, not liabilities.

Evolution

Following my retirement from the Navy in 2001, the speech went dormant for a while. I offered it to the companies that were kind enough to hire this old sailor, but as usual, time and money were barriers. I could not convince them that this seminar was a force multiplier—a concept that significantly increases "readiness" for life. The power and ingenuity of a joyful human spirit is amazing.

After eight years of retired military life and working in corporate America, it astounds me how little companies focus on their people! Business processes are important, but you need motivated, caring people to make those processes work.

In 2004, I landed a position with the Jacksonville Airport Authority helping put together the plan for Super Bowl XXXIX. This position was a direct result of my work as the military representative to the Jacksonville Super Bowl Committee during their bid to win the rights to the Super Bowl.

The Airport Authority found out about my motivational speaking experience and asked me to speak to many of their staff groups. I found my old message had the same effect on civilians. People are people, no matter what uniform they wear. They didn't just listen to me at VP-30 because I was a Captain or "Skipper." They listened because they recognized the value in the message and were buoyed by its positive perspective. The same was true for my new civilian audiences. It wasn't long before a good friend suggested I launch a website to help get the word out, thus, *andyandersen.net* was born.

So, that's my story; and here I sit on another airline flight having just delivered a talk in Lemoore, California to over five hundred sailors. I almost broke down as those sailors stood and applauded this simple message. One young sailor came to me afterward in tears and said, "I just had a terrible fight with my wife this morning over money. Thank you for changing my life."

I know I don't have the credentials of many, more-famous speakers, but I feel driven to change hearts and get America back on the caring track...back to the way this country was founded and shaped.

"Territory is but the body of a Nation. The people who inhabit its hills and valleys are its soul, its spirit, its life."

President James Garfield

Chapter II
Money and Materialism

Wow. Where do I begin?

I guess I decided this topic should follow "Evolution," because a discussion with a young sailor about the almighty buck started me on this journey in 1993. Money is the one thing most people chase their entire life. They are slaves to it, kill for it, and destroy families over it. It is, by far, the number one cause of divorce and domestic disputes. It definitely has caused a few disagreements in my house.

In 1985, Marty McFly went *Back to the Future*. He travelled to the year 1955, which is the year I was born. Back then, people were not bombarded with materialistic ideas by various types of media as we are nearly every minute of every day in today's world. And the message is so often the same—if you don't have this $50,000 dollar car, you won't be happy; if you don't have this 6,000 square foot house you won't be happy; if you don't have a wife who looks like this and drinks this beer you won't be happy. We are bombarded with this message so often that eventually we buy into it and waste precious heartbeats and risk broken relationships trying to capture the dream that society says will make us somebody and provide us with true happiness.

Why do we get so caught up in all these *things?* I love the quote by Lewis C. Henry: "Here's to our town, a place that buys things we don't need with money we haven't earned to impress people we don't like."[1] Money is a great tool, but a terrible master, and we need to understand that and keep it in perspective. It truly cannot buy happiness, but it is an essential part of our daily lives. I started my financial lectures because of the trouble the sailors and officers were having with credit card debt, car loans, and payday loan brokers. I saw the impact that poor finances can have on combat readiness and our fighting forces.

Back then, the general idea of my campaign was not where to invest to get rich, but how to stay out of trouble and live within your means. I wanted to change the materialistic mindset rampant within the ranks. Plenty of statistics back up the "he who dies with the most toys wins" philosophy. The savings rate in America for 2005 and 2006 was -0.7 percent. The last time we had a negative savings rate two years in a row was 1932 and 1933, during the Great Depression.[2] We are spending more than we make and many of us are likely headed for hard times as the baby boomers begin to retire.

Evidence of this is all around us. Consider all the foreclosures on homes bought with adjustable rate or interest only mortgages. These homes were purchased by people who truly could not afford them, primarily to give the impression of success. As we now know, banks and mortgage companies also are at fault for lending money to folks they knew were financially marginal with respect to buying high dollar homes. They too were motivated by *greed*.

An article I read recently pointed out that only 52 percent of Americans over age fifty-five have saved more than $50,000 dollars for retirement.[3] We all have read about the troubles with Social Security and that it is expected to remain solvent only until the year 2042.[4] At that time, unless changes are made, Social Security retirement benefits will need to be curtailed, which is particularly bad for those who are not saving.

I worked in banking for a while after leaving the Navy, and I remember seeing people, living on Social Security only, come into the bank at the beginning of the month to withdraw some money. They were not doing very well then. Imagine what life will be like for those people and many others who will follow in their footsteps if Social Security income is eventually limited or no longer available at all.

So what are the issues that lead to financial instability? I have a friend who was an executive with Toyota and he told me that America is the only country with a true market for Lexus, Infiniti, and Acura. Why do you think that is?

Could it be because Americans are the only people who will pay roughly $10,000 more for a car that is basically an upgraded Camry? That's right—the Lexus 350 is, essentially, a Toyota Camry with similar quality features and technology. I admit they add a few bells and whistles and change some cosmetics, but you are getting basically the same quality in a Toyota for a much more affordable price. Americans are willing to pay for that Infiniti, Acura and Lexus name. Yes, they are beautiful and well-made cars. I may even buy one someday— probably a used one. I'll be content to let someone else take the depreciation before I drive it for another two hundred thousand miles!

However, my financial situation is not the same as that of some of the folks in my audiences. My children's educations are paid for and I am pretty much set for retirement. There is no harm in buying one of these fine luxury cars when your other financial obligations are covered. But, it *drives* me crazy to see people who have not saved for their children's education or their own retirement cruising around town in $40,000 cars. One of the worst things you can do is put that kind of money into a depreciating asset.

A man came up to me at one of my lectures and proceeded to tell me that he had recently purchased a sweet Porsche Carrera convertible. I asked what he paid and he told me it cost him $95,000!

I said, "Wow! Did you just get a promotion?" Not only had he not gotten a promotion, he had been passed over twice. Upon further discussion, I discovered that his wife did not work outside the home and they were raising two kids. His response was, "But I got a great deal and the credit union will finance it at 4 percent for ten years!"

Let's do the math on this "great deal." On a $95,000, ten-year loan, the payments would be almost $800 a month before interest! The payment is astronomical to most of us, but the worst part, as I see it, is that this man could have been *earning* money with that $800 monthly car payment. Imagine the return on his investment if he had put that money in a mutual fund making a modest 8 percent interest while he drove a perfectly good and much more affordable used car!

An article I read mentioned that almost fifteen thousand Acura, Lexus and Infiniti nameplates were sold on eBay a few years ago. Apparently, the Honda nameplate can be peeled off and replaced with an Acura nameplate. Do you think we're into labels and status perhaps? I hope the people who bought those nameplates bought them to replace the ones that fell off their Lexus and not to improve their image.

I love the commercial for a national lender featuring a man talking about his nice home, vehicle, country club, and riding lawn mower and then saying, "How do

I do it? I'm in debt up to my eyeballs. Somebody please help me." A guy with a hundred dollar hat on a nickel head. Designer clothes with a Wal-Mart wallet.

When I was a kid, if I saw a Mercedes or a big home, I knew the people who lived there or drove that car probably had money. That is no longer true. We live in a materialistic society where fifty-year mortgages, interest only loans, and ten-year car loans are commonplace. Ten years is 12 percent of the average lifetime! We have to have that immediate gratification—now! America's paradigm of materialism is about to change as we go through this economic crisis. It is painful, but hopefully it will bring us to our senses.

Salespersons are trained to tap into your emotions. They want you to feel those supple, leather seats and breathe in that new car smell. They want to get you to take a test drive and visualize yourself in that vehicle, visualize your new image, and begin to think, "How can I make this happen?"

It can happen to any of us. In 1998, my son (USNA '01) came home on leave from the Naval Academy and wanted to go to the Washington DC car show to look at Mustangs. He would soon be getting his midshipman car. As we walked through the door, the first car I saw was a new 1998 Mercedes SLK 230 hard top convertible with a retractable roof.

Matt looked at me and said, "Dad, you gotta have that car."

I commented that the car must be $60,000 easy. I walked up and the sticker was *only* $40,000. Heck! I thought I just saved $20,000 dollars!

Then Matt said, "You're going to be commanding officer of the biggest squadron in the world and in Florida, no less, with its palm trees and sunshine. Just imagine how cool it would be to pull into your CO parking spot and put the metal top up. You only live once."

I found myself thinking, yeah, maybe he's right. I looked around and discovered one I really liked for $43,500. I even contacted a credit union that would arrange to finance it for seven years. My payments would be about $700 a month. I thought to myself, "If I reduce this life insurance and that investment I can afford that car."

My youngest son had not started college yet and I was three years from leaving the Navy. What was I thinking? I had been teaching this stuff for five years, yet, here I was being seduced by the *dark side of the force*. How easily we're pulled into the materialistic world.

As it often turns out, *what I needed was different from what I wanted*. One day shortly before I was to place the order for my Mercedes, I went to work out at the Pentagon Athletic Center and there, on a corkboard, was a 3x5 card that had been pinned up that very morning. It said, "1994 Mustang GT convertible, only 18,000 miles, garage kept, 5-speed."

Exactly what I wanted except it was a FORD—Fix Or Repair Daily—Found On the Road Dead. I could have a

Mercedes! I was getting caught up in exactly the mentality that gets folks in over their heads, severely restricts their financial future, and adds stress to their lives.

Please don't get me wrong. Mercedes are beautifully made and gorgeous cars. I recommend everyone enjoy such a car someday if possible, but only if you can really afford it and have prepared for a healthy financial future. My beautiful Mustang now sits in my garage, has 183,000 miles on it, and it's still on the original clutch, alternator, tailpipes, and water pump!

People often tell me their budget is too tight and they can't build up their savings or investments. I tell them that I can walk out in that parking lot and find money to invest. Had you purchased a used Civic or Corolla instead of that $35,000 SUV, your payments would be half of what they are and your fuel efficiency would be doubled!

Credit cards are the number two debt producer. I had my credit cards stolen last year, but I'm not going to report it because the person who stole them is charging less than my wife. (Just kidding.) I love that one from Phil Callaway's book.

But seriously, depending on the article you read, the average American carries about $9,200 in credit card debt.[5] They are basically borrowing on the future for something that often they really do not need. Now we have big screen, liquid plasma, nuclear, plutonium TVs that cost a small fortune and are out-of-date within six months. The technology exists to make things faster and better, but it is purposely withheld to keep the consumer buying the next advancement, one step at a time. That's how things work folks. That's what keeps our economy rolling and keeps you in debt.

A friend of mine told me about an acquaintance who bought a 5,000 square foot house and had two "fleeced" Cadillac's in the driveway—that's the term I use for leased. When he was invited to join his friends for a dinner out, he said he could not afford it. What's wrong with this picture?

Have you ever heard the story of the man who was going to hike the Appalachian Trail, but needed to pack his backpack before he could begin the hike? He started to load it with a sleeping bag, frying pan, a camera for pictures, a gun for bears, a flashlight, maybe extra batteries, an extra pair of dry socks, food, a book to read, extra matches for the fire, reading glasses, and so on, until his back pack was so heavy that he did not enjoy the hike.

Isn't that what many of us do with our lives? We pack them so full of stuff that the quality of our precious time decreases. I did just that in 1989 as a lieutenant commander living in Orange Park, Florida. My wife, Cindy, did not work outside the home and I had two growing boys. I decided we needed a new car, a new in-ground pool, and a hot tub for starters. Next thing I know, we were having trouble making ends meet. When that happens, the first thing couples do is start fighting, which has a terrible effect on their kids. Trust me on this one. Quality of life can suffer because of *stuff*.

In 1960, the personal self-storage business did not exist. Now America has between thirty and forty thousand storage businesses because we need a place to keep our *stuff*.[6] As a matter of fact, last night I heard Clark Howard (a superb financial advisor on talk radio) mention that there are more than fifty thousand storage businesses and some unfortunate folks are living in them due to the economic crisis. Do me a favor and travel light. Don't fill your backpack with too much *stuff*. By the way, I'm looking for a bumper sticker that reads, "He who dies with the most toys is still dead."

I am not promoting mediocrity and you should not feel bad if you own a luxury car. My point is you should set your priorities and take care of the really important things first. It doesn't mean you are a bad person if you own a Lexus. But drive it for a *loooong* time; and when you pay it off, invest those payments. If you have the means and you are financially comfortable with regard to kids, colleges, and retirement savings, go for it, if that's what you want. I just don't think folks understand the financial impact of a $35,000 car loan early in life. It is money spent on transportation supposedly to increase your self-worth while markedly decreasing your net worth.

Wouldn't it be great if we all could subscribe to the philosophy of a man who lived in 469 B.C.? Socrates said, "He is richest who is content with the least, for contentment is the wealth of nature."

"I don't read advertisements. I would spend all my time wanting things."

Franz Kafka

Living Well

My Money and Materialism Checklist
(List a few areas of your finances that are focused
primarily on materialistic pursuits.)

1. _____

2. _____

3. _____

4. _____

5. _____

6. _____

Chapter III
Simplicity

One of my favorite places to eat is a fast food restaurant called In–N–Out Burger. (Folks on the west coast can relate to this.) When you enter the place, you feel the way Marty McFly must have felt when he went back in time to 1955. The place is clean, the service is fast and friendly, the food is terrific, and the menu is incredibly simple—burgers, cheeseburgers, fries, and drinks. That's it. No specialty burgers, chicken sandwiches, onion rings, or hot dogs. Your choices are few, which simplifies the whole process, from placing the order to preparation and delivery of the food to the customer. And the food is better for it.

Dr. Barry Schwarz discusses this concept in his book *The Paradox of Choice, Why More is Less.* Dr. Schwarz presents the possibility that having so many choices does not necessarily make life better. As a matter of fact, he believes it decreases overall quality of life. The stress of having to research and decide between so many choices adds to the anxiety in our lives and introduces guilt about our failure to choose the very best option. Just start researching a computer or flat screen TV—wow.

I guess what I love so much about In–N–Out Burger is that it is such a pleasant break from the fast pace of life. In-N-Out Burger offers easy choices, quality food, and nice folks. It just makes you feel good.

I started this chapter with a west coast fast food restaurant because, to me, it is an example of one of the things we need to do in life to decrease stress and add happiness. Start recognizing and enjoying the simple pleasures and beauty that surrounds us each and every day—the smell of fresh rain, the incredible beauty of a flower, the sound of snowflakes hitting the ground.

This may sound strange, but as I age, I am beginning to see the true beauty around me. Colors are becoming more vivid for me, in spite of my steadily worsening eyesight. Perhaps my failing sight is offset by my growing heart. I could go fishing and not catch a thing and that would be OK because I would enjoy just watching the bobber and basking in the tranquility of the day and the momentary reprieve from the break-neck speed at which society moves.

I love the chapter in Phil Callaway's book, *Making Life Rich Without Any Money*, where he tells us that we need "someone" to slow things down. We don't need more megabytes, faster cars, or quicker microwaves. We need somebody who can figure out a way to slow life down and bring it back to a pace that does not take quality years off our lives. With all our advances in medical technology, we are adding years to our life but we're not adding life to our years.

One way I attempt this is by taking time to enjoy the little pond behind our house. I love to watch the ducks gliding gracefully across its surface. It took me a while to attract them with food and keep them coming back, and I love to watch them scoot across the water just as calm as can be while their little webbed feet are cranking away just below the surface.

The six ducks who hang around were born on a little island in the middle of our pond so I decided to name it Duck Island. Clever, huh? I also named the lake "Myers Lake," after the lake on *The Andy Griffith Show*, so Duck Island should come as no surprise. Oh how I love to spend evenings with my wife, just chilling in the back yard and watching nature unfold. It doesn't cost much to do these simple things and see God's beauty all around.

As you simplify, please take time to be kind. It just makes so much sense. Kindness is like honey. It's hard to spread it around without getting some on yourself. When we are self centered and mean spirited toward people, that attitude just manifests itself and spreads like a cancer. It makes our world worse. I just don't get why we keep heading in that direction. Please help me spread joy and goodness. I believe America's future depends on it.

I remember a trip back in 1999, when I was in the Navy. We flew to Canada for a professional, anti-submarine warfare symposium. It was February and very cold, especially for someone acclimated to Florida weather.

I decided to go for a jog as the sun was setting. The junior officers said, "Skipper, are you crazy? It's freezing out there and so desolate. Let's go have a Molson instead." We were at a remote base on the east coast of Canada. As I started my jog, I heard the snow crunching under my feet with each step I took. It was so quiet; I could hear the snowflakes falling.

You northerners know what I'm talking about. I saw a moose in the distance and he looked at me as if I were crazy, in agreement with the junior officers. It was such a peaceful run, and the simplicity of it just hit me. It is a wonderful gift if you can teach yourself to enjoy the simple things in life.

When I think of simple and peaceful, I think of our dog, Dusty. We had to put her down May 18, 2006. I will never forget that day as long as I live. So far, that was the hardest thing I've had to witness. That day I watched one of my very best friends die, and I wanted to be with her until the very end. She was such a loving and gentle dog and brought so much love to our lives. She taught us the true meaning of unconditional love. She was a tremendous blessing and the best $10 I ever spent. What a huge return on my investment.

Simplicity

It is kind of funny how things work out. My son and I were at an animal shelter in Massachusetts and had stumbled upon a beautiful Dalmatian. We decided to look over the rest of the dogs before we settled on her for sure, but within five minutes, before we could return to her, that Dalmatian was gone. I was so upset that I had missed such a fine dog by five minutes.

The next week, I decided to look at just one more shelter in Providence, Rhode Island. And there we found Dusty, our "wonder dog." We *wondered* just what she was. She had beautiful long blond hair and seemed to be a cross between a Collie and a Labrador Retriever. She had a perfect temperament and was full of love and patience.

Yep. That unconditional love is something to witness. A dog can be left alone all day on a hot porch and that tail will still be wagging when you get home. They don't give a rat's behind what your boss thinks of you and they love you to the ends of the earth, even if you mistreat them. I have a question for you…if you left your dog and your spouse in the trunk of your car for an hour…which one will come out licking your face? Just a thought. Dogs hold no grudges. There is a divine lesson in forgiveness and love to be learned from dogs. They forgive and forget, and love you for who you are. Maybe that's why "dog" is "God" spelled backwards. I just hope that God puts dogs in heaven to make it that much more heavenly.

Dusty is buried in the back yard now—just outside our family room about six feet from my easy chair. I still feel peace and love every time I see her grave. My life would not have been as rich without that four-legged companion and to this day, I have a pillow on my comfortable easy chair that says simply...

"My goal in life is to be the person my dog thinks I am."

Dusty the Wonder Dog, 1997

My Simplicity Checklist
(List the things that are currently complicated in
your life—items that represent your best opportunities
to simplify your own life.)

1. _____

2. _____

3. _____

4. _____

5. _____

Chapter IV
Relationships

Here is another critical topic that has an impact on the world and your happiness. As you know by now, I do not have a doctorate in Psychology. I certainly do not claim to be able to heal any of your mental issues, if you have any, with this book. However, I am a dad, a new grandfather, a former commanding officer who served with hundreds of wonderful sailors, as well as someone who has worked in the inner circles of Washington DC, traveled the world, and spoken to hundreds of audiences—as such, I have a few thoughts to share.

Relationships...this is where the rubber meets the road. Whether you like it or not, sometimes you feel like you can't live with people, yet, you know you can't live without them because humans are social animals; we are meant to be with other people. In John Ortberg's book, *Everybody's Normal Till You Get to Know Them,* he cites an Alameda County Study, headed by a Harvard social scientist, that tracked the lives of seven thousand people over a seven-year period. The study found that those who isolated themselves and were miserable with life were three times more likely to die at an earlier age than subjects who were more socially active and generally happier with life.[1]

Robert Putnam, in his book *Bowling Alone*, notes sadly, that we are experiencing a steady decline in social capital in this country—a general erosion of community spirit, engagement in the lives of our families and friends, and simple care for others. So here we go again with a "what's in it for me" mentality.

The *Journal of the American Medical Association* (JAMA) reported on an experiment in which 276 people were voluntarily injected with cold viruses. The people who were generally happy and were in healthy relationships were four times better at fighting colds. Evidently, meaner people truly are "snottier" people.[2]

So it seems that finding a compatible mate is good for our health. It is, by far one of the biggest decisions we make in our lives, that is, choosing who we want at our side as we walk the face of the earth. I start most of my talks with my background and jokingly say, "I'm married. My wife and I just celebrated ten years of happiness this year. We've been married for thirty-two years."

Usually, I get a good laugh and few stern looks from wives in the crowd. But I always follow that comment with the admission that I'm truly blessed to have the wife I have, and that I don't know why she puts up with me. I, like most people, have my share of hang-ups and shortcomings. It's amazing the comments I have made to the person who may be picking out my hospice bed.

My wife, Cindy, is my childhood sweetheart and one of the most positive, upbeat people I've ever met. She gets my message better than I do. If you are not happy with the person you come home to every night, life is miserable no matter how big your house may be or how much *stuff* you have.

It is not easy living with the same person for thirty-two years. We have had our ups and downs and I'm sure there will be more. It doesn't take long to learn that marriage, like any relationship, is based on give and take. In the beginning, you feel your heart flutter, toes tingle, and palms sweat every time you see the person with whom you are falling in love. You spend a significant amount of time holding hands and talking on the phone. Then, as time passes, feelings change and, hopefully, mature. At some point, it begins to require more thought and more commitment and decision.

One of the best quotes I've heard about marriage was from Robert Browning (1812–1889): "Success in marriage is not about marrying the right person; it's about being the right person." I've found that to be very true.

The more I work on my issues, the more my wife seems to work on hers. Most likely, you are not going to change the other person. They are who they are. Love them for who they are and work on that which you can control—making *yourself* better.

I also love a statement I heard on a talk radio show one day about an amazing phenomenon—our ability to shift our perspectives. No matter what kind of relationship you're in, if you think you're with the wrong person, try treating them like they are the right person, and they become the right person. It is a pretty cool concept and it works.

As a retired naval aviator, I know how tempting it is to lose sight of what we have, in favor of something else, something faster or younger. I am so blessed and lucky to be still married to the mother of my children, especially when I see the miracle of my grandchild and know the joy of sharing that experience with her. As many will attest, I'm very lucky to have her...I'm doing better than I deserve.

Brainyquote.com is a repository of famous quotes searchable by topic. I was browsing the site one day and found a quote attributed to J. Paul Getty: "I would trade all my billions for one happy marriage."

I realize a lot of folks reading this are divorced. My siblings are 75 percent divorced, but I certainly don't condemn them. I also realize that people get caught in bad situations and only they know what theirs is. You are a great person with incredible potential to impact hundreds of lives no matter what your marital status may be.

Relationships

My hope for you is that from this point forward you will work toward improving your relationships—with your spouse, children, parents, and friends. You must give-and-take, compromise, swallow your pride, apologize, surprise them with a gift, work on becoming a better person, and keep the magic alive. If you have children, please remain focused on them, especially if it becomes necessary to separate from your spouse. You, as a parent, have the largest impact on how they turn out, and they are the future of your family and of this country.

You see, most women "get it" better than most men do. Women often seek happiness through relationships while many men identify who they are by what they do and how much *stuff* they have.

Whether you are a man or a woman, if you do find yourself striving for power and wealth, please try to keep your relationships intact as well. You can do this by remembering from where you came, and that *self worth does not equal net worth.*

I know some wonderful, well-adjusted, wealthy folks, and I know some equally wonderful, well-adjusted, poor folks. They share a common trait—no matter how much money they have in the bank, they have kind hearts and care about others more than themselves. I love this quote by Pastor Paul Sheppard: "Love people and use money and don't love money and use people."

Please remember, you are not better than the next person because of your accumulated wealth. I hope and pray you use what you have for the greater good, share your blessings to further the American dream, and help those in need. He who dies with the most toys does not win. He who has a positive effect on the most lives is the real winner because, like Lily Tomlin said, "If you win the rat race you're still a rat."

You won't be remembered for your stuff; you will be remembered for what you did for people while you walked the face of the earth. You will be remembered for the footprints you left in people's lives. Caring is a basic leadership principle. I know the sailors I worked with could read through a heart in the blink of an eye, and the same is true for most people.

I can't tell you how many Navy leaders I've served with who, when speaking to a group of young sailors, would say something like, "Yes, I really care about you guys and your families, and, oh, by the way…we're going to go out and win all these military honors and awards."

Then I would go to lunch with those same guys and watch them treat a waiter like some sub-form of human life. Those guys don't really care about people, and no matter what they say, their true nature will show through because people can read hearts.

Let me share my long underwear story. I served on the John F. Kennedy as a catapult officer, shooting jets off the flight deck. It would get very cold off the Virginia coast where we practiced for deployment. We would endure 30-knot winds blasting across the deck in January. It was bone chilling.

I had just checked in to the ship with the Bow Catapults Division, which was made up of about seventy guys, none of whom were too fond of me because I flew an airplane that did not land on a carrier deck. From their perspective, what could a P-3 guy know about carriers?

One of the men came to my stateroom one night with my ration of long johns—five pairs. It occurred to me to ask how many pairs of long johns each of my men had.

"They have one each, Sir," was his response.

"So you mean to tell me when their one pair is in the wash they are on the flight deck with no long underwear?" I asked.

"Yes sir."

Let's see, is enlisted skin different than officer skin? I don't think so.

I told him to take those long johns back and not to bring me more than one pair until all of my men had more than one pair.

I did not share that story with a soul, but it spread like wild fire and earned me the immediate respect of the men. Simple consideration won them over completely.

"You see, it's true, people don't care how much you know until they know how much you care."

Anonymous

Living Well

My Relationships Checklist
(List some relationships in your life in need of repair.)

1. _____

2. _____

3. _____

4. _____

5. _____

38

Chapter V
Trifecta

When I was promoted to captain in the Navy, it was my last promotion in the military. I had the honor of having my new shoulder boards (rank insignia) placed on me by Secretary of Defense Bill Cohen and my oldest son, Matt, who was a sophomore at the Naval Academy. You can't get much farther apart in the military chain of command than that. I remember telling the crowd that day that my happiness did not rely on the shoulder boards or the size of my bank accounts (thank God), but was based upon what I called the "trifecta"— my faith, family, and friends.

The Andersens (L to R - Brad, Christy, Cindy, Andy, Brady, Stephanie, and Matt, 2007)

It's pretty basic stuff really but this powerful DC crowd seemed a little stunned by my statement. I guess they thought I would pontificate on the world's military situation, but I wanted them to hear what really mattered. It's funny how if you keep these things in focus, everything else seems to fall in place.

My purpose is not to get heavily into politics or religion, but I myself find great solace in connecting with a higher power. I have had too many awesome experiences not to believe there is a much better place ahead after this crazy time on earth. I feel this planet is a learning and testing ground for much bigger things in the next life. I often share my thoughts with others after my talks, if they want to delve deeper in this important area of my life. However, I would like to share one story with you.

A friend of mine, Captain "Turk" Johnny Green, died of esophageal cancer November 3, 2008. He was a wonderful American who commanded two aircraft carriers, and has a naval aviation memorial scholarship in his name.

A few days before he passed, he was in a semi-coma when, all of a sudden, his eyes opened; he looked up and said, "Wow!" That was his last word. The hospice nurse stood up and said, "I can't tell you how many folks look up and go out screaming."

That gave me chills.

Family. How much of our happiness can be drawn from this area of our lives if we could keep it in harmony? This is easier said than done, of course. I remember a line from the Tim Allen sitcom, *Home Improvement,* where Brad, the oldest of the three boys, wanted to go on a ski vacation with friends for Christmas instead of spending it with his family. Tim lets Brad know that, "Christmas is not about spending time with people you like. It's about spending time with family."

Isn't it funny how we tend to say and do things to those closest to us that we would never say or do to friends or co-workers? Our families are the very folks who will decide where we spend our golden years. Our family members will be primarily responsible for choosing our nursing home, or what I refer to as "God's waiting room."

This is something I have to work on all the time myself. My temper seems to have a shorter fuse around family, especially my lovely wife. Even so, I think our relationship is better than it's ever been. Of course, I am much more focused on it now, but for years, I just let it run on autopilot without much hands-on time. In other words, I put no time or effort into it; as a matter of fact, I neglected it.

Relationships take work and an empathetic philosophy. You listen and function from the heart, not superficially, as you see in so many relationships today. You've got to put your significant other first. I'll never forget when Cindy told me that I worked harder on my body than our relationship. She was right. I am a workout nut and I often chose workouts over doing something with her to strengthen our marriage. I figured it out and definitely re-prioritized.

I know you've heard the adage, you reap what you sow. Well then, why aren't we kinder to everyone? You never know how someone may come back into your life. For example, I've conducted numerous annual safety check rides in aircraft only to have the guys I was checking conduct my safety check rides just a few years later.

My point is, treating people well and with respect is the right thing to do, but it also is an investment in your future, because the time will come when you need either physical or emotional help; we all have rainy days.

Trifecta

When the time comes, money will not buy comfort or good will. I hope, when that day arrives, you will have sown your fields with kindness so that your crop will come back threefold when you need it most.

I worked with a gentleman at the airport on Super Bowl XXXIX in Jacksonville, Florida, and one day I asked him if he knew a particular individual with whom I was acquainted. He said, "Sure, I know him, but there was nothing he could do for me, so I have nothing to do with him."

I could not believe my ears. My thought was, "What if he needed something from you?" It's not about us; it's about caring about others! We have got to get this concept and get it soon. This "what's in it for me" mentality is going to kill the very heart and soul of this great nation.

"Our lives are shaped by those who love us."

John Powell

My "Trifecta" Checklist
(What areas of your Trifecta need work?)

1. _____

2. _____

3. _____

4. _____

5. _____

Chapter VI
Kids

Children are very important! They are the future of your family and they are the future of the United States of America. Our children did not ask to be brought into this crazy world, but they are here and they are our responsibility. *Nobody has a bigger impact on their outcome as human beings than mom and dad*—NOBODY!

Unfortunately, I believe parents are now more disengaged than ever in our history. The pace of life, stress, and the desire to have more is leaving our most important assets neglected in the dust.

Sunday afternoon flag football

One of the greatest times of the week around the Andersen household was Sunday afternoon in Orange Park, Florida. We developed a regular Sunday routine that was born of necessity during football season. The kids loved to play football on the front lawn and were tearing up mine with hours of play. I suggested they play in the street, like Bill Cosby did in his street football days.

My wife said no way unless I was out there playing with them. The boss had spoken. So I had the kids grab some socks to hang off their shorts and soon we were playing flag football. I'd play "all-time quarterback" and switch sides, although I was often accused of throwing interceptions to even the score. (I hated slaughters from either side.)

The next thing you know, the kids were putting black stuff under their eyes, I had to build goal posts, other dads came out to quarterback, and moms were bringing pitchers of lemonade to refresh the teams. It was quite a gathering of families.

I love this memory and often include this story in my group speaking engagements. I've been told that some who have heard this story went home and started their own street football league with the neighborhood kids, and it is just as awesome and fun for them as it was for us. This kind of gesture can rekindle many father-son relationships in those little neighborhoods. My kids still remember those times as some of their greatest childhood memories, when we all came together and spent time with our most valuable investments (them), because T – I – M – E is how a child spells love.

They want your time. I love the quote by Fyodor Dostoyevsky, "The soul is healed by being with children."

An article I read mentioned that most childhood education experts agree that a child's character and mental make-up or personality begins to form at the pre-school age.[1] They need discipline and love before and after this time. If either one of those gets out of whack, there is a pretty good chance you'll have problems. Have too much love without discipline and you may end up with a dependant, "boomerang" adult child who can't hold a job and has no sense of responsibility. On the other hand, a child with too much discipline and a lack of love may grow up to be insecure and emotionally unstable, searching for love in all the wrong places.

Please give them both. They deserve it and you owe it to them. In the Navy, I spent quite a bit of time on six-month deployments, so when I was home I did not want to be the bad guy. As a result, most of the discipline fell to my wife who did a wonderful job. I have two very fine sons. I guess I would say I was the fun guy and my wife was the disciplinarian, for which I give her credit today. My boys respect what we each brought to the table.

Also, try not to discipline in anger, as I have been known to do on occasion. Your judgment is poor when you are angry, so a word of caution: calm down and gain some perspective before addressing difficult discipline issues.

Human touch is also very important. In his book, *Everybody's Normal Till You Get to Know Them*, John Ortberg mentions that hospitals hire people as "baby huggers" to care for, hug, and touch children who have been abandoned. Researchers have found that a child is not as emotionally stable without being held and having the benefit of love and the human touch.

I would also ask you to try to keep your inevitable "discussions" with your spouse out of earshot of the kids. I know my parent's arguments had an emotional effect on me and my siblings in that little neighborhood on the south side of Chicago. This is a tough one, especially when you lose your cool, but I still say *one of the best things you can do for your kids is love your spouse.* Please remember that one.

All of the articles I have read that mention divorce and the divorce rate now place the percentage of marriages that end in divorce as exceeding 50 percent across the United States. Because of this, I realize a large number of the people in my live audiences, as well as those reading this book, are divorced.

Still, the same concepts apply to divorced parents. Divorce does not excuse you from dedicating your love and time to your most important asset, your children. You still must ensure that your children are raised with a loving foundation. If anything, this is more important to children of divorce, because the divorce not only affected you and your former spouse, it had a tremendous emotional impact on your child, your flesh and blood, your legacy. You provide the basis for their developing personality and success. Please don't put them behind from the beginning.

My hat is off to our school teachers. God bless them! Due to the rising number of domestic issues, pace of life, and stress, discipline and basic values are not being taught at home like they used to be. We are putting this burden on our teachers. I heard a teacher on the radio say he spends forty-five minutes on discipline and fifteen minutes on math. Wow. They already have their hands full with just trying to teach our kids in this fast-paced world.

I hope this is sinking in before it's too late. We're already seeing the repercussions, with low tests scores, fewer students majoring in technical subjects, and increasing dropout rates. I beg of you to engage in your children's lives.

Every child, actually every person, needs to feel a sense of self worth. The vast majority of people who take their lives do it because of a general lack of self worth. In Phil Callaway's *Making Life Rich Without Any Money*, he mentions a gripping example of this with the suicide note of a teenager. The suicide note said, "You gave me everything to live with but you gave me nothing to live for." I pray you never have to live with a statement like that for the rest of your life.

Please remember, *"Your kids are a living message to a future you will never see."*

John Whitehead

My Kids Checklist
(What are some things you can do to further
your children's potential?)

1. _____

2. _____

3. _____

4. _____

5. _____

Chapter VII
Suicide

I realize this does not sound very motivating, but it should be when I finish—because you may save a life someday.

Suicide has touched my life so many times and in so many ways. One of my best friends in high school was supposed to attend the Naval Academy with me in 1973. Instead, I attended his funeral on May 3, 1973. I will never forget that day. He hung himself in his parent's home. He left no note and seemed to have everything to live for.

Years later, a friend of my son's who was supposed to go to the Academy with him, shot himself while home on leave. Talk about history repeating itself.

A chief petty officer I knew while I was in command, slit his own throat. I stood in his blood, hugging his sobbing wife a few hours after his death. One of my good friends, an airline pilot, took his life a few years ago. He left behind a wife and three beautiful children.

A former senior chief petty officer in my last squadron took his life just recently and, while I was on active duty, the Chief of Naval Operations apparently took his life. I could go on, but I think you get my point.

The website suicidology.org reported this year that in 2006 more than thirty-three thousand people in the United States took their own lives. Every year, that number increases. These people decide what their exit date will be on their gravestone. And, active duty military are twice as likely to take their own lives as their civilian contemporaries.[1] While I worked for the Secretary of Defense, a retired two star Army general took his life at home. Suicide has no respect for wealth, age, gender, or fame.

According to the childtrendsdatabank.org website, suicide is also the number three killer of teenagers after auto accidents and homicides. It is becoming an epidemic.

Please remember the teenager's suicide note to his parents near the end of Chapter VI. Hopefully this will motivate you to cherish time with your kids, go to their T-ball games, read their report cards, and be there when they need a hug. That's the reason I talk about such a morbid subject, because the crazy pace of life, economic collapse, and rising family issues are increasing the suicide rate.

As a deacon and Stephen Minister in my church, I've had some training in dealing with people—how to look for suicidal signs—and learned how to listen and care.

Suicide

The bottom line is heart. People are starving for what John Ortberg calls "joy bringers." These are people who can make others feel that life is worth living and that they have meaning just in being themselves!

You can save a life by looking for certain signs such as a lost job, divorce, financial problems, losing weight, depression, and someone who no longer looks you in the eye, to name a few. The most basic instinct a human being has is the will to live. When someone is considering ending it all, his/her brain is not functioning correctly. You can save someone's life by caring and staying connected with your family and friends' lives. Let them know that you are happy they were born.

I went to the gym at Naval Air Station Jacksonville to work out one day, and standing over in the corner was a very impressive looking and, as we say in the Navy, "squared away" senior chief. That is the second highest enlisted rank in the Navy. I did not recognize him, but he called me over and said, "Andy, I just want to thank you. I was going through an ugly divorce with deep financial problems and considered ending it all, when I attended one of your seminars. You changed my life. Thank you."

You never know the impact you may have, or how you can make a difference.

A woman who was training me for a banking position once quoted the following line, and I never forgot it. It's worth remembering.

"Suicide is a permanent solution to a temporary problem."
Phil Donahue

My Suicide Awareness Checklist
(Who might be on your suicide watch?)

1. _____

2. _____

3. _____

4. _____

5. _____

Chapter VIII
Forgiveness

Funny, but I was in the process of making my final edits to this book and still praying I could somehow get it published when the word "forgiveness" popped into my head. So, I scrolled through the text, knowing I must have put a chapter on forgiveness in here somewhere, and discovered it was missing. I wasn't sure where it would end up in the book but just know this, it may have been the last chapter I wrote, but it is clearly one of the most important.

I once heard Joyce Meyers speak. She said that holding a grudge or just plain hating someone and refusing to forgive is like drinking poison and hoping that the other person dies. It doesn't bother them in the least.

When you can learn to forgive and move on, it is like lifting a huge burden off your back. It frees your mind and spirit to affect more lives in more positive, meaningful, and sincere ways.

You see, once you hit about age thirty, your body starts to decay. My fifty-four-year-old decaying, acne-scarred, graying, arthritic, borderline Type 2 diabetes body is strictly a transportation vehicle to get my spirit to your spirit so that we can interact with each other. The cars that we buy to make us look good are really a way to get our spirit, and those of our friends and family, together faster for that interaction.

I have had some relatives and friends hurt me very deeply, but learning to forgive them and move on has provided me with a renewed spirit of forgiveness and peace. It was not easy and even with practice, it still is difficult to forgive others, but it is essential to continued happiness.

One of the biggest obstacles to forgiveness is that old "p" word—pride. I've heard many preachers say it is the biggest sin of all because it leads to all the other sins. It gets in the way of all relationships, especially marriage, and makes people not want to forgive but rather get even, or maybe ahead.

What makes us so anxious to hold on to that grudge or hatred when we ourselves are guilty of also hurting so many? I can't begin to remember all the pain I've inflicted, whether with or without intent, through the years. An excellent biblical lesson on forgiveness can be found in John 8:7, where a woman is brought before Jesus and accused of adultery. Her accusers state that according to the law, she must be stoned. Jesus agrees and says, "If anyone of you is without sin, let him be the first to throw a stone at her." They all leave, one by one.[1]

As my pastor says, "We're all a mess," or as Opie Taylor would say, "We're a sight." The sooner we realize the reality and depth of God's love and forgiveness, the sooner we become free and able to move in the spirit of forgiveness for all.

One of my toughest challenges has been to learn to forgive myself. I believe you must first be able to forgive yourself before you can forgive others. I have done many things I am not proud of and I hold myself to higher standards than I do others. I sometimes am amazed at my blessings, considering all of my transgressions against others. I truly am doing "better than I deserve"—a line stolen from famous financial counselor Dave Ramsey. I draw great strength from famous biblical and world leaders who also have stumbled, but still had a very positive impact on many lives.

So let's forgive ourselves, count the blessings we don't deserve, forgive our friends and family, and lift those grudges that stand between us and the peace of the spirit that we need so desperately to share. It will make your life better, and in turn, will better the lives of those around you. That's just how it works.

As I write this chapter, I am on a plane from Reno to Dallas, looking out of my window at the landscape of this great country. America is going through the worst financial crisis since the Great Depression.

The need for the American people to forgive themselves and each other is great. We need to find a way to lift our burdens and clear the way for more peace and the ability to affect more lives positively. I have been talking about this for almost fifteen years—about focusing on what is most important. The timing of this message could not be better. This country is in for a spiritual and materialistic cleansing that we have desperately needed. America needs your forgiving spirit. Please help me make it happen.

> *"People are often unreasonable, illogical and self-centered;*
> *Forgive them anyway."*
>
> *Mother Teresa*

My Forgiveness Checklist
(Whom do you need to forgive?)

1. _____

2. _____

3. _____

4. _____

5. _____

Chapter IX
Prejudice

One of the pleasures I've had in the last few years is working on Naval Aviation's Diversity Program as a contractor. I know some of you may be rolling your eyes and thinking, "Here we go again with equal opportunity, counting numbers, quotas, and so on." Well, I quickly found out that the true gist of diversity is not equal opportunity.

I'm particularly fond of a quote from Dr. Samuel Betances, a recognized international consulting expert on diversity from Chicago who said, "Diversity is not about counting heads. It's making heads count." In other words, every person has worth and brings a different set of skills and talents to the table. A truly diversity-focused organization will nurture each person and cultivate every individual's strengths.

I have always believed there is good in each person, but as life and the environment around folks unfold, much of that goodness is masked and buried. Nonetheless, we all have it in us. It's just buried a little deeper in some people.

The word prejudice comes from the words "pre" and "judge," and its meaning is derived from those two elements. In other words, prejudice refers to the process of making a judgment about the type of person someone is based on superficial characteristics such as outward appearances, affiliations, music preferences, belongings, the type of car he/she drives, sports teams he/she supports, and the like. It is the act of judging others prematurely, before we really have a chance to get to know the person.

This often is a harmful and almost always wrong assessment. You never really know the heart underneath that outward appearance that people tend to present until you get to know them. As a Cubs fan, I'm sure I've been pre-judged as a sports nitwit or a brooding, pessimistic loser. I just answer my accusers by saying, "Hey remember...any team can have a bad century!"

I have a couple of stories to share to illustrate my point.

Much of what you have read so far is simply a compilation of things I've seen and heard throughout my life. This story is no different. I gave a talk at the Mayport Naval Air Station a few years back. Afterward, a young sailor came up to me and relayed the following story.

He said a friend of his, a fellow sailor, had purchased a brand new Ford F-150 pick-up truck and was driving it on the beach (as we can in some Florida counties). The sticker was still on the side of the truck when he got it stuck in the sand with the tide coming in rapidly.

He attempted to get someone to help him pull it out for about forty-five minutes to no avail. Finally, he noticed an old beat up pickup truck coming down the beach. It slowed as it neared him and the driver stopped his truck and offered assistance.

However, the appearance of this good Samaritan made the stuck sailor a little suspicious. The man was dressed in biker garb with tattoos and earrings. "Great," the wayward sailor thought. "I finally get someone to stop and help and this guy is going to take my wallet."

Still, the young sailor took him up on his offer and watched as the "biker" fellow positioned his vehicle, hooked a chain between the two chassis, and quickly pulled the new F-150 out of the surf, just as the salt water began to lap against his transmission.

The very grateful sailor thanked the man profusely and offered him $20 for his trouble. The rag-tag-looking, helpful soul simply said, "I don't want your money. Just help the next person who needs it and don't ask for anything in return."

As it turns out, the man who stopped to help the sailor in distress was a petty officer first class, United States Navy, and a master at arms (military police officer) to boot!

Living Well

The point of this story is that the sailor in distress took a prejudicial view of the man who stopped to offer assistance based solely on outward appearance and dress, when in fact this man was his angel of mercy. This is the "pay it forward" concept so beautifully portrayed in the Hollywood hit film of the same name from a few years back, and a philosophy we all should adopt.

Back in 1998, when I was working for the Secretary of Defense, I decided to attend a three-day Christian men's retreat in the mountains of Maryland. When I arrived at the retreat lodging area, I was greeted by a man with long hair and tattoos, dressed in biker attire, who proceeded to take my luggage out of the trunk. I thought, "Hmm, someone must have hired this homeless guy to carry luggage and make a few bucks."

Boy was I wrong. I soon found out that my "porter" was probably the most inspirational speaker of the entire weekend. He was the president of Christian Bikers of America. Talk about eating crow and feeling small; what a lesson learned.

Along the same lines, about every six weeks I deliver my motivational address (the contents of which you are reading) to a homeless center in Jacksonville, Florida called the City Rescue Mission. The City Rescue Mission clothes and feeds the homeless, and helps them prepare résumés and get back on their feet and into society. A few weeks before they graduate from the CRM program, I give them this speech. One of the first times I did this,

Prejudice

I remember looking at some of those guys and thinking, boy I would hate to see them in a dark alley.

At the end of my talk, I asked for comments and thoughts. I was, and am, so humbled by the power of their testimonies as they shared what they had been through and how they, at that moment, looked at life. You can learn something from everyone.

After I talk to the group, I give them a copy of Phil Callaway's book, *Making Life Rich Without Any Money*, and I write on the inside cover, as I've said before, "Net worth does not equal self worth." We all are here for a reason and we all can have an impact.

You really don't know the heart that beats within the person whose outer appearance you are judging. That man or woman has seen their share of troubles and been molded by who-knows-what kind of environment or set of circumstances—maybe molded to carry a message to you, to be there with you for a divine appointment, and make a difference in your life if your heart is open.

Assume the best, look for the good in people and please don't pre-judge. You just never know what kind of spirit lies inside that unique set of genes.

"The show doesn't drive home a lesson, but it can open up people's minds enough for them to see how stupid every kind of prejudice can be."

Redd Foxx

My "Pre-Judge" Checklist
(What prejudices do you need to clean out?)

1. _____

2. _____

3. _____

4. _____

5. _____

Chapter X
Listening

We live in a world of talkers and people are in need of good listeners.

As a Stephen Minister in my church, we train for six months so we can learn how to help people through life's crises. I would have to say the central theme throughout the course was listening. We even kept a little sign on our desks that had the word "fix" on it with a red encircled "X" emblazoned over the top. The message was "don't try to fix the problem, just listen with your heart."

I'm not sure where I read it, but I heard there are five types of listening and I'm pretty sure my wife accuses me of several of these on a regular basis, especially when I'm watching football:

- Ignoring
- Pretending
- Selective

- Attentive
- Emphatic

Emphatic is where she wants me to be and where I hope you will move to, if you're not already there. That means you listen with your heart—you really focus on the person speaking and let him/her know that you really care and are interested in what he/she has to say. At that moment of his/her need, this is the most important person in that room to you. Your eye contact and body language are critical to conveying your concern.

When my wife and I go out to eat, she always races to the table to ensure all I see is her and a wall to help me keep my eyes focused on her. She thinks I may have attention deficit disorder, as I often tend to scan the room. I say I'm just like a gunfighter and like my back against the wall. I think you get my point.

My New Year's resolution this year was not to finish people's sentences, but to let them talk. I definitely am a Type A person. I am almost always thinking about the next thing that I'm going to say instead of really listening. I'm getting better at curbing that tendency and really listening. Of course, it has taken years of training and practice.

We tend to have trouble remembering a person's name just minutes after being introduced, because we are so busy wondering if we said our own name right, if our hair looks right, worrying about whether there is something hanging from our teeth or nose, or how we are coming across and what we should say next.

Listening

I can remember giving a talk at a men's prayer breakfast and at the end of the talk, a man approached me with tears in his eyes and wanted to discuss a suicide in his family. Instead of looking him in the eye and giving him my full attention and concern, my eyes were scanning the room for my pastor because I had something I wanted to tell him. I regret that incident to this day and have since apologized.

The art of listening is especially critical at key moments in your children's and spouse's lives. When someone in your family is hurting and needs your love and attention, that person will never forget it if you are not able to focus on their needs when it is most important. Likewise, they will always remember that you were there for them if you were able to find the focus they required.

When my oldest son, Matt, was about twelve, he went through a period of insomnia. He came into our bedroom in the middle of the night and said he could not sleep. I had an early flight the next day and instead of being patient and giving him an Andy Taylor to Opie talk, I lost my cool and yelled at him to get in bed. I regret that incident to this day. What an opportunity lost. I have since apologized to Matt.

So, don't have regrets, and develop a habit of listening emphatically now. Consciously work on it every day. It's just that the pace and stress of life is taking away this skill, as folks just don't seem to have the time to sit and really listen.

Living Well

Listening relates to the chapter on suicide. If you remember, I mentioned the number one cause of suicide by far is the feeling of lack of self worth. If you know someone who has these thoughts and comes to you for advice or companionship, listening will be the best way for you to let that person know you care and will always be there. That's what people want to know—that someone truly cares and that they do have self worth.

If you master the art of listening, you will be more successful in everything you do and will have more friends than you can *shake a stick at.* It seems pretty simple, doesn't it? But as you practice, you'll see it takes work and concentration before it becomes second nature. However, once it does, people will notice a beautiful change in you and they will want to spend more time with you, which will make you and the world around you a much better place.

"Life is short and we never have too much time for gladdening the hearts of those who are traveling the dark Journey with us. Oh be swift to love, make haste to be kind."

Henry Frederick Amiel

Listening

My listening Checklist
(List the tools that can make you a better listener.)

1. _____

2. _____

3. _____

4. _____

5. _____

Chapter XI
Gossip vs. Compliments

One of my favorite television shows of all time is *The Andy Griffith Show*. Not only is it entertaining, but it also makes you feel good and warm inside, unlike most shows today. In addition, it almost always leaves you with a lesson about life. I was watching an episode the other day in which Andy walks into Walker's Drug Store and notices Aunt Bea in the corner with a group of ladies, who seem to be having a very good time. Andy comments, "You ladies look pretty happy; must be cutting somebody up pretty good."

This is a very easy trap to fall into and I venture to guess that almost all of us have done it at one time or another. I once heard gossip described as "dishonest self-praise." A great description because it makes us feel better to trim someone else down and expose their faults when in fact most of us are full of our own issues.

I'm willing to bet good money that those with whom you gossip are all over you like a "cheap suit" when you're not around. It takes great strength of character to go against the grain and see the positives in the person being skewered, or simply just not join the feeding frenzy. I truly believe there is good in each person and we were born that way. When I look at my beautiful grandson, I can't believe he has any prejudice or evil in him yet. That is taught by his environment, which is exactly why our role as parents have the most critical impact on how our children and grandchildren are shaped for adult life.

I think the words coming out of our mouths are kind of like toothpaste—easy to squeeze out, but once they're out, it's impossible to get them back in. Words can be so cutting, as sharp as a razor blade, as we cut someone's heart out. When you say nasty things to or about other folks, it's your spirit damaging their spirit. That's why it hurts so badly.

I think one of the worst sayings I have ever heard is, "Sticks and stones may break my bones, but words will never hurt me." Wrong! Your wrist or ankle will heal eventually, but I can remember, as I'm sure you can, some very hurtful things said by friends, relatives, and immediate family...scars on our hearts. It doesn't matter how long ago it was either, because they're permanent.

I urge you to think before you speak ill of others; I'm speaking to myself, as usual, as much as to you. When you brush your teeth, brush your tongue too and get some of that nasty stuff off before it slips out and hurts someone you love.

Gossip vs. Compliments

You know...it's kind of like you carry an emotional ATM around with you at all times. You make either deposits or withdrawals from those you meet and talk with, and many of them you may never see again in this life.[1]

This is not a dress rehearsal for the next time you get to visit this tiny spec in God's great universe, so maximize your time by making others feel better. As I've said, by doing this, you make your own life better. Think about how a simple thing like someone smiling at you warms you, as opposed to the feeling you get when someone gives you an old scowl or dirty look. It can make the difference between an emotional deposit and a withdrawal. The brightness of your spirit is a direct reflection of the balance inside. Someone who has marital problems, hates his neighbors, or is brow beaten at work will reflect a low emotional balance, indeed. The balance sheet can be read on a person's face. In other words, your face is a reflection of the health of your spirit.

When I get up in morning and have some quiet time to get my mindset right before I attack the day, I remind myself to compliment at least three people genuinely that day.

It is so much easier to talk bad about folks than to lift them up. Watch people's expressions when you say something kind like, "You have a very bright spirit and a wonderful personality. Never lose that. America needs it."

That person will just beam with an inner joy because you just stoked their coals! What did that cost you? Nothing...and, often, it pays.

Living Well

I remember going into a Burger King in Patuxent River, Maryland to indulge in one of my weaknesses. I needed, well wanted, a chocolate milkshake. I walked up and read the girls nametag and said, "Lakeisha, you have a bright spirit; I would like a milkshake."

She responded, "You know you're the first one to use my name this week and you pronounced it right. Would you like a free shake?"

"Yeah, I'll take a free shake." All it cost me was taking the time to use her name and smile.

In the last squadron I commanded before retiring, I used a very effective tool to motivate folks, besides the speeches. The troops called them "red zingers." Commanding officers in the Navy write in red ink to convey a sense of urgency to the recipients. The executive officer first writes in green as a warning. If the green warning is not heeded, a red may follow.

One day, I heard about one of the sailors who had taken a Saturday night watch for a shipmate whose pregnant wife had developed complications. I thought that was a noble and selfless gesture, but it didn't quite warrant a Navy Achievement Medal.

So I began to ponder how I could recognize him. I decided to take about ninety seconds to write him a thank you note on my personal stationary, and in red ink, of course.

I also believed in leadership by walking around, or LBWA. So, I had occasion to visit his spaces not long after the note. On the visit, I saw he had placed my note in a frame on his desk for all to read. It was then that I realized that "little" things really mean a lot to people.

Then, the squadron maintenance officer reported on the stellar performance of his parachute riggers on a recent inspection. I was always impressed with their professionalism when I visited them to get my survival gear before I flew. So, another "red zinger" went out.

The next time I flew, I saw the note up in a prominent place for all to see. A small amount of my time made a big impact on the troops—a big return on a small investment.

People do well with positive encouragement, but not very well in negative environments. You can only beat a sled dog so long. At first, it may seem to work. He'll run fast initially, but eventually he'll lie down. The more successful companies understand this critical concept to long-term success by leading with genuine care rather than intimidation.

Why are we so prone to complain instead of compliment? One time, after I had consumed a beautiful and tasty Whopper with cheese (another weakness), I decided to let the cooks know just how much I had enjoyed my meal at their fast food restaurant. As I walked out, I pointed to the minimum wage guys in back and said, "That was the best Whopper I've ever had!"

They looked at me as if I were crazy. I said, "Well, how many times have you heard how you messed it up?"

"Oh we hear that all the time," was their reply.

Living Well

I know most of you have called the manager or let your waiter/waitress know you were disappointed with your meal or the service at some point. I want you also to start making the effort to give positive feedback.

I recently was in a fast food restaurant in Meridian, Mississippi called Penn's, and thought the food and service were superb. I decided to approach the counter and tell the manager. As I asked for the manager at the counter, the woman standing next to me said, "Oh, hold my order; I need to know what not to order."

I asked her why she assumed I was going to say something negative, and she responded, "Well, that's what most people do."

I rest my case. You see this new approach soon will become second nature and those folks at your favorite restaurants will get even better at what they do and treat you like you own the place.

Nothing but good comes out of this mindset. I realize many of you get this, and are practicing it already, so keep up the good work. And those who are brooding complainers...take on a new face. Everyone, including you, will love it. If you are happy inside, please let your face know it!

"I can live for two months, on one compliment."

Mark Twain

Gossip vs. Compliments

My Gossip / Compliments Checklist
(List items to work on to compliment more and
gossip less.)

1. _____

2. _____

3. _____

4. _____

5. _____

Chapter XII
Mayberry

I considered naming this chapter "Being a Good Neighbor," but decided to name it after the town of Mayberry, where being a friendly neighbor is commonplace.

Yes, I know, Mayberry doesn't exist. Although I did go to the "Mayberry Days" event in Mount Airy, North Carolina. It's Andy Griffith's hometown and the basis of many of the characters, places, and shops depicted in the show.

It was pretty close to the small town depicted on *The Andy Griffith Show*. It had that same peaceful air about it. But I must confess; much of that atmosphere was attributable to the wonderful people who attended the festival—people who loved *The Andy Griffith Show* and got what it was all about. They knew that it is a mindset, a way of life, and knowledge of how we wish life could be—simple and slow-paced, where people care about each other and accept and love everyone, even the town drunk. That's what makes a place like Mayberry so special.

Even though it does not exist, why can't we strive for it? In my speeches, I love to tell the story of how some say Mayberry came to be. The way I tell it, Andy was sitting on his front porch and a fellow stopped his car in front of the house and said, "What town is this?"

Andy said, "Why, this is Mayberry."

"Well, what *kind* of town is it?' asked the stranger, to whom Andy inquired, "What kind of town did you come from?"

The fellow in the car said, "It was not a very nice place. The people were mean, the stores were terrible, the sun never shined, and the roads were bad."

Andy said, "Well this is the same kind of town so you best keep moving."

A little later, another fellow pulled up and asked the same question, "What kind of town is Mayberry?"

Andy wanted to know what his last town was like and the man responded, "It was beautiful, folks were great, the sun shined often, and the stores were terrific."

To this, Andy replied, "This is the same kind of town. Why don't you stay?"

You see, it's an attitude thing, a mindset.

A military friend told me that he saw the Jerry Springer Show broadcast in Baghdad. Of all programs to be seen by the people that we are supposed to be helping, is this the kind of society they would want to adopt? Is this the kind of image we, as Americans, want the rest of the world to see?

You won't see *The Andy Griffith Show* over there. The sad thing is that we promote and support shows that expose the ugly side of people's lives, and we seem to feed off it. It's all about ratings and money. There are more judges on TV now than beer commercials. Those shows are just another way to feed people's hunger to see pain in others' lives. Please don't let your kids watch those shows because it affects them in such a negative way, and they may very well begin to think those lifestyles are acceptable.

Almost every house in Mayberry has a front porch. In the Old South, before air conditioning was commonplace, homes had front porches out of necessity. The houses got so hot from the day's heat that people would sit outside at night waiting for the house to cool before they went to bed. Everyone on the block did this, so they actually got to know their neighbors.

"Hey, Gomer."

"Hey, Goober."

I venture to say most of us don't go to the trouble to get to know our neighbors these days. Why do I need to know my neighbors? If I need a cup of sugar, I'll just order it online and have UPS deliver it the next day!

If you cultivate relationships with your neighbors, I bet you will enjoy your neighborhood much more. Cindy and I have developed a few habits over the years to help us get to know our neighbors. We take a plate of hot, freshly baked chocolate chip cookies to new neighbors, introduce ourselves, and let them know we are available if they ever need anything.

That simple gesture and $3 investment has an amazing effect on people. I also enjoy just putting out a simple flyer around holidays to organize potluck picnics in our cul-de-sac. Everyone tends to bring their favorite dish and it does not cost much, but the benefits are immeasurable, and we all get to know our neighbors. These are the kinds of things that seem to be dying on the vine, and it's sad because they make life better.

When I go for a neighborhood jog, I notice fewer people return the waves *I initiate*. That's not only unfriendly, but also rude. Years ago, almost everyone would return a wave. When I get out in the country, I don't need to initiate the wave because country folks wave at me and I love it. I'm betting things are simpler and slower out there. I rest my case...again.

I purposely built a big front porch on my house. I love it when people say, "Your house is so inviting." They call it the Andy Griffith house. That's how I want people to feel, warm and welcomed. Put a front porch on your house and you won't regret it.

One of my neighbors, Tom Gloe, works for UPS and has one of the most infectious, joy-filled laughs I've ever heard. I love his jovial nature. A few days after he moved next door to me, I walked over to borrow something. He looked at me with that great big signature smile of his and said, "Mi casa, es su casa, neighbor." Or, in English, my house is your house. I wish we could all adopt that philosophy.

Do me a favor and be a better neighbor. It truly is a win-win situation. I love the scene from the sitcom *Home Improvement* where Jill is in the backyard talking to the kind and philosophical neighbor, Wilson. Tim comes out and says he needs to go to work and has to talk to Wilson. Jill says, "We only have one Wilson and I'm using him."

Tim then comments on how bad he needs to talk to Wilson and he doesn't know how long he can hold it. Finally, in exasperation Tim gives up and says, "Well fine! It's off to work I go, without my Heidi-ho."

I actually have a neighbor as kind and smart as Wilson. His name is Garo Mavian. He always has a kind word and time for you no matter what he is doing. I even call him "Wilson." He understands what it means to be a good neighbor and I often go to him to get my "Heidi-ho."

I hope you understand the gist of my message here and never have to go off to work without your "Heidi-ho" and please remember...

"Without friendships no one would choose to live, even if they had all the other good things in life."

Aristotle

Living Well

My Mayberry Checklist
(List things you can do to make your neighborhood
more like Mayberry.)

1. _____

2. _____

3. _____

4. _____

5. _____

Chapter XIII
Driving

It seems I've written much of this book on airplanes and in airports. As I write this chapter, I am sitting in the Nashville airport, having just arrived from Raleigh-Durham. I spoke to three hundred Marines at New River, North Carolina on this trip. I had at least ten Marines lined up afterward to speak to me, and most asked for a book or something to take with them to refer to as their life unfolds. So, I press on!

One indicator that stress is getting the best of us and that society may be headed off the deep end is our driving. It seems to be getting worse.

Driving is the most dangerous thing that most of us will do. In 2005, 43,200 people died on our nation's highways.[1] They were moms, dads, brothers, sons, sisters, and daughters. People often talk about the tragedy of the war in Vietnam, where we lost fifty-eight thousand of our nation's finest during a ten-year period. Well, we lose forty-three thousand of our family members each year on our highways. So why in the heck would you make it worse out there by continuing to spread an "aggressive driving" cancer that kills more and more people? Again, it is by far the most dangerous thing most of us will ever do in our lives.

I guess I may have a few daredevils or carrier flight deck folks in the audience. It's funny how we talk of fear of flying or possibly being killed by terrorists, but never think twice about jumping behind the wheel of our cars, even when we are angry or distracted. The chances of having your name on one of those little round signs along the side of the highway are much better than most of what we fear.

Yes, driving is a necessity in today's mobile society, but we could make it much easier and safer for everyone with a few good habits.

I think seat belts have become pretty much ingrained in our brains and wearing one is the law in most places. I have a co-worker who refuses to wear one. He'll let that seat belt warning alarm just go crazy rather than buckle up. I try to tell him it wouldn't take much to launch him forward and crush his face against the windshield, but my efforts are in vain—which reminds me of the story of a police officer who spoke at one of my squadron's safety stand-downs.

He came upon a vehicle stopped along a quiet city street. He stopped and approached the car to find a women crying and holding her lifeless toddler in her arms. He asked what happened and she said a dog had run in front of her vehicle forcing her to slam on her brakes. The child, who at the time, was standing in the front seat unbuckled, was thrown forward against the windshield and the impact broke his neck. Please, I beg of you, the kids know no better. At least give them a fighting chance to have a long life. You owe it to them.

The best hint I can give to improve driving in this country is to practice consideration for other drivers on the road. One way to do this is to stick a little closer to the speed limit. I occasionally drive 5 to 10 mph over the limit, but I find more and more that puts me in the category of having blue hair with just my knuckles showing on the steering wheel. In other words, most folks are blowing by me, weaving in and out, just asking to create a multi-car accident. What is the big hurry? There must be a lot of rich people out there who can afford all those tickets and increases in their insurance rates!

Another way to show other drivers consideration is to allow them to merge. Very few people these days move over or slow down a little to allow folks to merge.

"I'm not going to let you merge; I'm going to get there 3.5 seconds ahead of you because my time is more important than yours!" For what—to just process food, to not be engaged in your kids' lives, to neglect your marriage, to ignore a hurting neighbor? I guess I don't get the hurry.

I still flash my lights to let truckers know that their back end is clear and they can move over. Occasionally, they will flash back to thank me and then I flash back to say, "You're welcome." Not only is it a good feeling we share, but it increases the level of safety on our highways and gets more of that good karma going. However, I have noticed that the number of truckers who thank me is steadily decreasing as they speed by. Hmmm... I wonder if that too is an indication of the "direction" we're heading.

The other day, I let a gentleman who was turning onto my main road go ahead of me. As he merged in front of me, he rolled down his window and held out a sign that said "Thank You." I loved it! I hoped the light would turn so I could get out quickly and tell him how much I loved the gesture, and that I was going to add his wonderfully kind action to my speech and book. I also wanted to ask where I could get one of those signs and to see what was on the other side had I not let him in! I was never able to catch him, and a later search of his neighborhood did not turn up his little red truck. However, after 6 months I finally found him the other day, his name is Derry Lewis, and folks say he runs the most honest Auto Electric and Air Conditioning business in Jacksonville, Florida. That's no surprise. And by the way, I just had my own sign made...thanks for the idea, Derry.

I have a friend who was once the maintenance officer for the Navy's flight demonstration team, the Blue Angels. He told me about an incident that occurred

Driving

while in New Orleans for an air show. As luck would have it, one day he was out in the unfamiliar city in his rental car and before he knew it, he was lost. He was confused and anxious and he accidently cut someone off in traffic. The man he cut off became very upset.

My friend said he suspected that the other guy probably would have killed him if he'd had a gun in the car. The language and gestures emanating from the man's vehicle were horrendous.

As they approached a tollbooth, my friend decided to pay the $2 toll for the upset man behind him. Once they both had cleared the tollbooth, the other man passed my friend, rolled down his window, waved, and said, "Have a nice day." Situation diffused for a mere $2. The moral of the story? Pay someone's toll; it may save your life!

So, let's slowdown, be more courteous, let folks merge, flash those lights, and cultivate kindness on our highways. It will lower your stress level, make you happier, and maybe you will even live a little longer for it.

"Let's wave people in with all our fingers instead of waving them off with one!"

Andy Andersen

My Driving Checklist
(Things I will do to be a more courteous driver.)

1. _____

2. _____

3. _____

4. _____

5. _____

Chapter XIV
Patriotism

I am very proud to be an American. It is not because I spent the best years of my life in the Navy. It is due to the sacrifices I've seen, how we care about the world around us, and, by the way, our lifestyle is pretty darn good.

One of the great gifts of military service is world travel. I have very much enjoyed some countries. I loved Scotland; Canada was beautiful; Israel was probably the most fascinating place I visited, with China and Italy close seconds; and Australia was chocked full of fun-loving and kind people.

But America is my home, and we do many things well here. I know we have our issues, but every culture and country does. One of our most endearing qualities is our sense of justice and our willingness to lend a helping hand when the world needs it—no matter where or when it's needed. The blood of our forefathers has been spilled all over the beaches of this world for the last two hundred years so that we could make a difference for freedom and peace.

Now it is not my intent to get into world politics and I know there are many mixed feelings about things we have been involved in near and abroad. I certainly do not know all that goes on behind the decisions in DC. My point is that America has almost always reflected the heart of the message in this book.

Please put your political views aside and just try to understand where my heart is coming from. I hope you have felt your heartstrings tugged a little bit as you have read these pages, as it is heart that is really the foundation of my message. I'm afraid we're losing heart in this country and perhaps the world. September 11, 2001 changed our world. But, we still seem to be driving faster, wanting more, building bigger houses and smaller families, losing patience, not smiling as much, and less willing to lend a helping hand.

We can't lose heart. That is what America was founded upon. The "what's in it for me" mentality is a deadly cancer that is spreading throughout our country and it is making things worse for all of us! By treating others with kindness and caring, we promote good will and positive karma, so to speak. That actually makes others feel better about themselves and you.

I will never forget, as long as I live, the opening scenes of the movie *Saving Private Ryan*. That was one of a few movies I have seen where no one moved or spoke at the end of the film. Those opening shots of soldiers storming the beaches at Normandy were horrific. Many of those who were there said the scenes from the movie were very realistic. One veteran who was there said, "The gunfire was so intense as the door of the landing craft was lowered, it mowed down all the men in the first row; I had to push the bodies of my friends out of the way to get to the beach."

Amazing...he literally had to step over his friends bodies to get to the beach. That's what I'm referring to—selfless dedication by Americans. Young men and women answering the call to serve and giving every-thing—never to have a family, go fishing with their grandchildren, or even just see their homes again. They did it for peace. They did it for you and they did it for me. I will always be eternally grateful for their sacrifices.

My then 17-year-old son, Brad, sat next to me dur-ing the film. You know 17-year-olds; they know every-thing. After the movie, I asked him what he thought. He looked at me and said, "Dad, it makes me want to be a better American for what they did for me." Yes! What a great thing to say.

More than a million Americans, 1.2 million in fact, have given their lives in the same way. Men and women are dying or having limbs blown off in Iraq and Afghanistan as I write this.

One of my prized possessions is an American flag my oldest son, Matt, had with him on his aircraft

Living Well

during several combat missions in Afghanistan. Yes, his mom and I did some worrying, but we also knew he was doing his part, as so many had before him. We're glad to have him home and are very proud of his service.

The least we can all do is follow Brad's comment, and be better Americans by treating people kinder and caring about each other more. It's true; the vast majority of us will never have the opportunity to do what they have done. We won't be in that life and death situation in combat. We won't be asked to make that sacrifice.

Our police officers and firefighters also put their lives on the line daily, but most of us do not. The least we can do is honor their deaths, and be more caring and involved citizens to make this country better than we found it. It's within your power and does not cost a dime.

The other thing we take for granted in America is our abundance. Let me throw a few statistics at you for those who think they don't have enough *stuff*. Depending on which article you read, if you have any money in a savings account or change sitting in an ashtray at home, you are richer than 92 percent of the world.[1] As a matter of fact, of the six billion people walking this tiny spec in the universe, three billion live on less than $2.50 a day. According to UNICEF, twenty-five to thirty thousand children die each day due to poverty.[2]

That peaceful rest we enjoy, whether it is in a doublewide mobile home or a 6,000 square foot brick home, was paid for dearly. The ability to pursue happiness, the freedom to worship whatever we want wherever we want, the ability to walk into fully stocked grocery stores, hike through our gorgeous national parks, or fish with our families truly makes us rich. We all should cherish these freedoms. Please help make a difference for those who gave it all so you and I could enjoy this wonderful lifestyle. Let this book sink in and enlarge your heart like that beautiful scene from one of my favorite stories, *The Grinch Who Stole Christmas.*

"America is the last best hope for this world."

Abraham Lincoln

My Patriotism Checklist
(Things I will do to show I care about those
who died for me.)

1. ————————————————————

2. ————————————————————

3. ————————————————————

4. ————————————————————

5. ————————————————————

Chapter XV
What Can I Do?

I realized something important one day—I can't remember when or where it was, but I believe it was about the time I was asked to become a caregiver to hurting men in my church and about the time I picked up Phil Callaway's book on how to make your life rich. Those things happened in 1998, and it was sometime during that year that I reached a conclusion. I experienced one of those nights when I could not sleep, because I could not turn my brain off. I was lying in bed listening to my heartbeat and I realized that I only have so many of those left until I'm out of here.

This is not a dress rehearsal for the next time. I knew my chance of making admiral and affecting more lives through the Navy were pretty slim for a P-3 pilot. I figured I was probably a typo on the captain's list for that matter.

I also realized almost every financial move I had made had gone in the direction opposite my intentions. I was a buy high sell low kind of guy. So I knew I probably wouldn't be a millionaire someday and be able to buy a shelter for the homeless. I was left wondering what I could do with what time and talent God had given me.

Then it occurred to me. I could try to be the best husband, dad, son, brother, neighbor, church member, driver (well there is a novel idea...let someone merge!) and co-worker I could possibly be. You get the idea. It does not cost a dime to have a very positive impact on almost everyone with whom you come in contact. It is all in your heart and attitude. You will be in the minority and may appear *abnormal* to many folks, but hopefully your infectious newfound personality will have an effect on many people and make a difference before you pass on from this world. This new concept will also be something that the Joneses most likely do not have, and it's free and it improves your life.

I hope by now you've picked up a few tidbits and pointers about how to be a positive influence on those around you. One of my favorite things to do is pay someone's toll...like the story of my Blue Angel friend. That is definitely abnormal. I often travel to Orlando where there are a number of toll roads, and I enjoy the reaction I get when I pay for the person behind me.

I will approach the booth and give the man/woman a dollar for a 50¢ toll. He/she will shove 50¢ back at me, and I then mention that I want to pay the toll of the guy behind me. The toll attendant always smiles and thinks that's pretty cool. Chances are he/she will end up telling someone else about it, thereby spreading the good will. I watch in my rearview mirror as the hands fly back and forth between the attendant and the next driver. They inevitably will point to my old red mustang.

Yep, that's the guy who did it. Then I will deliberately keep my speed at 55 miles per hour knowing that the guy will pass me. You get one of three types of folks: a Navy pilot who will pull behind you hoping you pay the rest of his tolls; a guy who comes by and gives you a thumbs up and a smile (now he may very well mention the incident to his friends); or the guy who gives you a sneer or a strange look like you're some kind of weirdo. When that kind of guy exits, he looks in his rearview mirror to see if you're going to follow him. It's just a fun thing to do and it makes an immediate impact for minimal cost.

Here are a few other abnormal tips:

- Always ask for your waiters/waitresses name. Asking "Tim" for more bread as opposed to "hey you" gives your server a sense of self worth, makes you look better, and improves your service. It is such common sense, but many people just do not get it!

- Compliment the cooks as you walk out, even if it's fast food. Everyone needs to know that he/she is valued.

- As you stand in your grocery checkout line, read the cashier's nametag before it's your turn to check out. When the cashier says, "Welcome. How are you today?" you can respond with, "I'm fine, Jennifer. How are you?" Jennifer will be surprised and pleased that you took the time to notice and use her name. It changes the entire conversation and promotes the same caring atmosphere as with the waiter/waitress. Also, make the bagger feel as important as the store manager because, in the end, he really is.

- When I give my little motivational talk, I hold up an old nail or screw and ask the audience to name it. They always guess the object easily. I say, "Actually, this is a very bad night for a single mom with two small kids in the car at Wal-Mart at 9:00 p.m. on a rainy night. She has a flat tire. You could have saved her that trouble if three months ago you took 1.5 seconds during your jog or walk to lean over, pick it up, and dispose of it." You could pick up hundreds if not thousands in a lifetime of walking and jogging. It's easy to do with a big potential impact.

- Hold doors open for people. So what if they get to the counter before you. Slow it down. I had a friend who often wore his biker garb around town. He said it was funny to see the look of shock when he held doors open for people, and women often moved their purses to the opposite side of their bodies. Are we judging a book by its cover perhaps?

- If you are not financially strapped, over tip your server, especially at Christmas. The folks who take your groceries out, cut your hair, or serve your food are not doing it for their health, and often, they cannot afford to eat out themselves.

- Smile at people. Most will smile back. Notice how a baby smiles back and they do not know you. They don't even know how to talk yet, or what the smile concept means, but their spirit "gets it."

- Flash your lights to let truckers know they are clear when they pass. If they flash a "Thank You," flash "You're welcome." They work hard keeping the economy "rolling."

- Please wait your turn when standing in a gaggle to get something. You know who got there first (like at a deli with no numbers). I love Stephen Wright's line that he was arrested for scalping low numbers at the deli. You may even consider letting someone go ahead of you if time permits.

- Pay for the bill of the person behind you in the fast food drive-thru. I did this at McDonalds the other day and as I watched my rearview mirror, I noticed the person behind me paid for the next car! Pretty cool. I heard a story from a guy at my last seminar about a Starbucks somewhere in the Pacific Northwest. They had some kind soul who paid for the guy next in line and the chain he started lasted for days. Wow!

I'm sure you can think of other *abnormal* things to do. I just hope this gives you a few ideas and gets your creative juices flowing. It's fun to be abnormal. And, remember, this type of behavior used to be normal. People really cared about other folks in a world that will always be in desperate need of kindness. As I said before, you reap what you sow; and we are sowing a very bad, selfish cancer that will come back to haunt us. Perhaps when you are in one of the valleys of life, you will need someone to help you. I hope you get what I am saying and start adding to the positive and good side of life.

When I had the revelation about what I could do, I decided to change my lecture and focus more on life than money. I wanted to see what kind of impact it would have on the new squadron of twelve hundred souls with whom I was about to have the pleasure and honor to serve. That philosophy had a much greater impact than I imagined, and I hope it reaches your heart today.

"The great use of life is to spend it for something that outlasts it."

William James (1842-1910)

My "What Can I Do" Checklist
(notice I doubled this one)
(Things I will do to make me "abnormal.")

1. _____

2. _____

3. _____

4. _____

5. _____

6. _____

7. _____

8. _____

9. _____

10. _____

Chapter XVI
Random Acts of Kindness

I debated about whether to include this chapter. I dislike sounding "braggadocios," if there is such a word. When you do something good for someone, you're not supposed to tell anyone. I believe this is because, on the opposite end of the spectrum, when we do stupid or shameful things, we try to hide them. I have more than my share of those unpleasant stories. However, I think it appropriate, considering the message this book is intended to convey, to tell you about some of the things I have done and witnessed that were positive. It may make it easier to find those moments in your own life. It's also intended to tug on your heartstrings a tad more.

Besides really connecting with my God or my wife, few things make me feel better than helping someone in need. Let me run a few special moments by you.

- One night in the late 1980s, I was driving home in a rainstorm in my 280Z (it was ten-years old with one hundred thousand miles on it) with a load of groceries. I was in my flight suit and in a foul mood for some reason. I saw an old black man, who must have been in his sixties, pushing everything he owned in a shopping cart down a very busy road in Orange Park, Florida. I remember thinking about how much prejudice and pain he must have seen in his life. A little voice inside me insisted I go back and give him some money. I did a u-turn and stopped in the parking lot he was transiting. I pulled a ten-dollar bill out of my wallet, put my arm on his rain soaked back, and handed it to him. I said, "Sir, I want you to have this. How are you today?"

  He replied, "I'm just fine and feeling blessed. How are you?" I realized that he had a better attitude than I did and look what he was going through. It's funny how moments like this kind of "re-cage our gyros," as we pilots would say, as we rethink our priorities.

- In December 2006, I was in the Naval Air Station Jacksonville commissary shopping with my wife. As we stood at the checkout stand, an older woman in front of us was going through the checkout line. When the cashier finished putting all her items through the register, the elderly woman pulled out a bunch of coupons. The cashier said they no longer accepted those particular coupons. So the woman slowly started to put things back—soap, paper towels, a Christmas ham—in an effort to get her bill down to what little she had.

My wife noticed what was happening and said "Bob (my real name), do you see what's going on?" I was oblivious to it because I was lost in thoughts of the upcoming Bears playoff games. Cindy said, "Help pay her bill."

I told the cashier to put the woman's overage on our tab. The cashier stared at us in disbelief and said, "But sir, it's seventeen dollars." I assured her that was fine. It was a small amount to a retired sailor with another job as well, but a huge amount to a woman scraping everything she had together so she could put food on the table.

The elderly woman shed a few tears, hugged us, and wished us a Merry Christmas. But the really neat thing about that whole experience was the effect it had on the people who saw what happened. Many of the baggers in the vicinity commented on it, saying how wonderful it was and that they would not forget it. When you do these things, they make you feel better, and of course, those who receive your kindness, and anyone else who witnesses the acts, get a little lift as well.

- Speaking of Chicago Bears games...at the end of the 2006 season, when the playoffs were set, I got a call from my son, Brad.

"Dad, I found tickets to the playoffs on eBay. Let's go to the Bears-Seahawks playoff game." Knowing the Bears poor recent playoff history, I was not overly enthused about leaving my sunny perch in Florida to brave the frigid Chicago weather. But I thought, even if they lose, what a great bonding opportunity this will be with my son.

Brad and I rode the train into town for the game. We arrived early. While we were tailgating, eating sausage sandwiches, and drinking very cold sodas and beers in 20°F temperatures and driving snow, I spotted an old homeless man rummaging through the trash and collecting our empties to recycle for a few pennies. This sight broke my heart and I felt guilty for the scene I witnessed— the haves and the have not's. I took $20 out of my wallet and handed it to him. It was a quiet exchange, as he thanked me and moved on. Brad and I proceeded into the game and the Bears won in overtime. I don't believe I have ever hugged more strangers in my life than I did that day.

As we left the stadium, Brad and I went back to the spot where we had tailgated to pick up our chairs. A hand grabbed me from behind and a well-dressed gentleman in a very expensive leather jacket said to me, "You're the good Samaritan."

"What do you mean?" I asked.

"My group saw what you did for that guy and we were touched. Thank you."

You just never know how far reaching the effects of your gestures of kindness will be. Brad wrote me a letter when I was at a three-day men's retreat recently and told me that he would never forget that incident.

I love the Liberty Mutual commercials showing people helping each other and performing small acts of kindness. Each person's kind gesture is witnessed by another, who is moved to help the next person in need that he/she encounters. If that is truly Liberty Mutual's core philosophy, it sure sounds like a great company culture. It is right on target with this message.

- A couple of years ago when I was working on Super Bowl XXXIX at the airport, I remember stopping at a gas station for gas, a diet coke, and a Krispy Kreme doughnut—the breakfast of champions! As I left the station in my car, I saw an obviously homeless man walking toward the building.

I remember him because there was a horrid growth coming out of one eye. It looked like he had lost that eye. I could not even look at or acknowledge him like I normally would because he looked so grotesque. As I drove to the airport my little voice started working on me. "I can't believe you did not even acknowledge that man, especially at Christmas. There was a human being behind that face."

After driving almost ten minutes away, I returned to the station hoping to find him; and there he sat on the cold cement. I pulled $20 from my wallet, handed it to him, and wished him a Merry Christmas. His fist came forward to hit my fist (like the NBA guys do at the free throw line), and with a tear coming out of his good eye he thanked me. We two souls who did not know each other connected for a very brief moment in our lives.

- On a recent trip to Wrigley field, where my Cubs again got into the playoffs and failed to show up, I noticed a sad scene. Two blind folks with red canes, husband and wife, were trying to get out of the stadium with no obvious help. I watched as the woman accidently put her red cane between an unsuspecting woman's legs. She tripped and turned around with a look of disgust. I thought,

"Lady, do you see what is going on here? These people are blind!"

I told my boys to stand on the curb and that I would be right back. After a fifteen-minute walk, I got the couple to their train station. I must say I was disappointed in the number of folks who passed them by—some of them my beloved Cub fans! Do not miss opportunities like that. Please, as we used to say in naval aviation, use SA (situational awareness).

• On a recent business trip to Los Angeles, I missed the San Diego freeway south exit. At the time, I was headed away from LAX airport, down I-5 South. Yep, I was on the cell phone with my headpiece and missed my exit (bad thing to do). Unlike most men, this time I pulled off and asked for directions. As I was rerouting and heading back to the airport, I saw Central Avenue in south LA, which reminded me of one of my favorite old television shows, *Sanford and Son*.

I remembered that Fred and Lamont lived on Central Avenue in south LA. I had a little time and decided to check it out. Yes, I could see why they chose that area for the show's supposed location. It was definitely a poor area of LA, and not too far from where I was born in Hawthorne.

As I sat at a light, I saw an old Hispanic woman selling flowers and, I believe, cherries. She had an elderly man with her and two small kids. I motioned her over to the car and she brought her wares. She spoke no English. I waved off her products and just handed her $5. She ran back to her group jubilantly waving that $5.

That was $5 dollars well spent. My heart smiled. My only regret as I approached LAX was that I did not give her more.

- I recently heard a great story about the commanding officer of Naval Air Station Jacksonville, Captain Jack Scorby. Skipper Scorby was in a tire place for an oil change when he overheard a mechanic tell a woman with small kids that her car needed more than an oil change. Her two front tires were unsafe. She said she simply could not afford two new tires. You guessed it…without her knowing, who picked up the ticket? Captain Scorby paid for her tires. How awesome! That is a humble servant attitude. As we say in the Navy, "Bravo Zulu, Skipper."

- I once offered $10 to a homeless man in Jacksonville. He was happy to take it, but as I held it out, I started to get second thoughts, so I asked him, "How do I know that you're not going to take this and go buy a twelve pack and get drunk?"

He said he had given up booze many years ago and was very hungry.

I asked, "Well, how do I know you're not going to get a lady for the evening?" He mentioned that he did not need any diseases on the street.

Then I asked, "Well how do I know you won't go rent some clubs and hit balls at a driving range?"

He said, "Are you kidding? I gave up golf after I lost my home ten years ago!"

I said, "I tell you what, I'm going to keep the ten dollars and I want you to come home and have dinner with my wife, Cindy, and I."

He said, "Are you kidding me? My clothes are ripped up, I smell, and I have this disgusting, crusty beard."

I said, "No, that's OK I want her to see what happens to a man when he gives up beer, sex, and golf."

I'm kidding. That is a joke I stole from a sermon by a local pastor. It's not true, but the rest of these incidents are. I just wanted to bring a little smile to your face.

I could relay countless other stories of events in which I have witnessed others give a few dollars to people begging on the streets. The amount they gave probably depended on the amount of money they had on them or their assessment of the situation.

Some of the folks I see asking for money look pretty darn healthy and young—able to work at least for minimum wage. So I guess I'm somewhat selective. Folks have often told me that I'm just supporting an alcohol or drug habit. But, what makes any of us so arrogant or judgmental to assume that we know this person's story?

I'd rather err on the side of good and assume they are just in a tough situation. If they do buy a twelve pack, oh well. At least they had a night when their pain was numbed on me.

I know I've been blessed and I intend to share to the best of my financial ability. I also believe in supporting worthwhile organizations when I know most of the money will go to those in need. Be careful, there are plenty of scam artists out there, but I'm pretty good at recognizing genuine pain and hunger. If I make a few mistakes, that's OK. I feel pretty confident that most of my donations landed in a growling stomach.

Please remember, most of the time you will receive no thanks and no one will see the good things you do. However, that's OK. That's not why you're doing it. You are doing it because it's the right thing to do, and you are sharing your blessings. Besides, I know it's being registered somewhere.

"God does not comfort us to make us comfortable, but to make us comforters."

John Henry Jowett

Living Well

My Random Acts of Kindness Checklist
(Random acts of kindness ideas)

1. _____

2. _____

3. _____

4. _____

5. _____

Chapter XVII
Happiness

Happiness can be elusive. From what I've read, Americans seem to be more unhappy than ever before. We now have more conveniences and time saving devices, yet, we seem also to be more discontent. Why do movie stars and multi-million dollar athletes, who appear to have everything, seem to be searching for something more?

The word happiness actually derives from the word "happen" or, in other words, what happens to us. So we spend most of our lives trying to acquire things in an attempt to find that happiness. One study showed that the difference in the levels of happiness between a homeless person and someone with a doublewide and a pick-up truck is substantial. However, the difference in happiness levels between the owner of a 1,500 square foot house and someone who owns a 5,000 square foot house is minimal. People get used to higher incomes and bigger toys. I do not care how many things you have, if your relationships are not in order, life is miserable.[1] An old Chinese proverb says, "A man can have 1,000 beds but can only sleep on one." It doesn't matter how big your house is if you're not happy—life is pretty tough.

It's funny, but once you have the basic human needs like air, water, food, and shelter, more stuff or money does not make you that much happier. Actually, having and maintaining more things can cause stress levels to rise and lead to greater discontent.[2] Researchers have found that most people who win the lottery and leave their old neighborhoods for a big home or remote ranch somewhere are actually less happy than they were when they lived in a 1,500 square foot house and coached little league. Henry Ford once said, "I was happier when doing a mechanic's job."[3]

I gave my talk on the USS John F. Kennedy before her last cruise. A master chief came up to me afterwards, shook my hand, and said, "Andy, that quote by Henry Ford just changed my life. I love to work on motorcycles. That's my passion and that's what I'd like to do when I get out of the Navy. I don't want to climb the corporate ladder and go after that big house. I want to pursue my passion and be happy with what I have."

Please don't get me wrong, I am not promoting mediocrity. Happiness can be found in that big house, but keep money and stuff in perspective. You can be very happy with a lot of material items, but don't let those things own you. Keep your priorities right and focus on what really matters in life.

There is a song by country singers Brooks and Dunn called the "Dirt Road." The lyrics of this song are about the fact that "happiness is not reserved for just the high achievers." Be happy with or without *stuff.*

According to wikipedia.org, the average United States median income in 2006 was $48,000, so most people in this country won't make CEO or COO income. They'll be common folk, so to speak, and won't ever get to that six-figure income, so learn to be happy wherever you are. That is the bottom line.

You can't pick your parents or the situation you were born into, but we do make many decisions that affect our lives. So, do the best you can with the cards you were dealt, and enjoy every breath you take. What are your other options? Be miserable until the day you die? As they say at Hospice, "Every day is a gift."

Speaking of Hospice, I am a hospice volunteer. As such, I have been witness to the stories of many people nearing the end of their lives. I remember one man's story in particular. I was talking with him and asked him if there were any lessons that he could share with me. He struggled to speak through his plastic oxygen mask and said, "Well not really. My Air Force career was lousy. My first marriage was a disaster, and my current wife does not care about me. I haven't spoken to my only son in twenty years. He doesn't even know I'm dying."

Wow, folks, that is not where you want to be when you check out.

Hospice has taught me two things. The first is not to fear death. I've seen the transition and how well the people from hospice care for their patients; and before I know it, I'm going to be in that bed. All of us will get there eventually. So I'm going to make the best of my time *before* I reach that point. My goal is to die young as late as possible. I love the Jimmy Buffett line, "I'd rather die while I'm living than live while I'm dead."

The second is that so much of our happiness is between our ears—our attitude. One of my favorite people was a man named Ken Graham, who worked at the Naval Air Station Jacksonville. Ken was a gray-haired, older gentleman who bagged groceries at the commissary. One day, I was leaving the commissary in my flight suit with Ken behind me, pushing my groceries. I was headed toward my 1994 Mustang (with one hundred fifty thousand miles on it) and I was in a foul mood.

But old Ken was whistling away as he walked behind me. He was just happy to be alive. I turned to him and asked, "Ken, why are you so happy all the time?"

He replied, "Well, Captain, when I get up in the morning I have a choice. I can choose to be happy or choose to be miserable. I choose to be happy." Ken just died April 11, 2009. He bagged groceries that morning and left us that afternoon. He added so much joy to people's lives.

Happiness

What many of us also fail to remember is that everyone has issues. The only folks without issues are dead. When is the best time to be happy? Today! It seems like we all wish we could just have __ (*you fill in the blank*); if we could only have that one thing, we could find happiness.

I can remember going through the commissary in Pensacola as a young ensign with a new baby thinking, "Boy, I can't wait until this kid is out of diapers. That will save me twenty dollars a week. Then I'll be happy."

Then, when he was six or seven years old, I found myself walking through the commissary thinking, "Boy, this kid is getting into everything—breaking stuff, getting gum and candy all over everything." (I call kids "stickies" because they always have some kind of sticky substance on them like gum or candy.) "I can't wait until he's older. Then I'll be happy."

Then, the next thing I knew, he was a teenager. He was talking back to me, messing with my car and girls, and occasionally my beer supply. I thought, "I can't wait until this kid is out of the house. Then I'll be happy."

Then he was attending Florida State and costing me $1,200 a month, and I thought, "Boy, I can't wait until he's out of college. Then I'll be happy."

Well, I paid off his college loans in December of 2005, and now I am facing the decreasing health of our aging parents. Before I know it, it will be my turn to enter the dying phase.

We will all be in that hospice bed and the blood will start to withdraw from our extremities to protect our vital organs. Then our breathing will become shallow and rapid, then there is a last wisp from our mouths, and we're gone. Remember there is almost always something with which we must cope, and if we aren't careful, we will waste all of our years thinking things will be better...when?

Now is the time. We don't get a second chance at this crazy thing we call life. I believe it is a dress rehearsal for heaven, but not for a second chance on this planet...so give it your best shot today.

I have had my attitude adjusted on many occasions. One incident occurred while I was driving to work on I-295. I was a lieutenant commander, so it was around 1989 or so, in Jacksonville, Florida. I was headed to the base in my flight suit and I was dreading the day for some reason.

As I passed a bus that said "Pine Castle" on the side, I looked up at the big windows of the bus. A woman inside with Down's syndrome looked down at me and gave a warm smile and a wave. I thought, "Look what she deals with and how happy and kind she appears to be. Maybe someday I can do something for them."

When I got to work that very day, there, on my desk, was a contribution form for the United Way and the Combined Federal Campaign. I looked to see if Pine Castle was a possible recipient of the donation money.

It was on the list and was described as a training facility for adults with disabilities.

Not only did I send a check, but I also included a letter explaining the smile and wave I saw that day, plus a few words about how every human being deserves the best life possible. I received a wonderful personal letter from Executive Director Jon May in response.

As my naval career progressed, I had the honor to command a couple of squadrons and I did not forget Pine Castle. Every Christmas, I would invite all two hundred Pine Castle clients to our squadron for refreshments, tours of aircraft, and flight demonstrations. As you can imagine, they were thrilled. But I had another angle. I knew the effect that these wonderful, loving, people would have on the sailors.

Many of our visitors needed physical assistance so I had the officers and sailors support their movements throughout the squadron. They could see how happy these people were in spite of their infirmities. I even saw tears in the eyes of some of my more "salty" sailors and chiefs.

I also made sure that the news crews from local TV stations were there to broadcast the touching event. I am not sure who it impacted more, the people from Pine Castle or the troops. It was a beautiful way to make a difference. My naval aviator son, Matt, decided to carry on the tradition with Pine Castle and his first squadron VP-45. It made me very proud.

Living Well

As I mentioned earlier, as a hospice volunteer I meet many people near the end of their lives, and I hear their last thoughts and comments. I've never heard any one of them mention that they wanted more money, but they all wish they had more time. Many people in that situation want to know if their time was well spent and whether they made a difference.

There is a movie called *About Schmidt*, starring Jack Nicholson. In my speeches, I ask the crowd if anyone has seen that movie. Not many have.

In the beginning of the film, Nicholson portrays a retiring insurance salesman who is being honored for his years of service. At Schmidt's farewell dinner, an intoxicated co-worker in the crowd lets him know that the company could care less about him. But, our hero has his gold watch and is feeling pretty good about himself.

A few weeks later, Schmidt returns to his office to retrieve a few things he left behind and finds all his paperwork and personal items have been boxed up and thrown into the alley. In addition, the young man who now occupies his desk proceeds to tell him that the programs he (Schmidt) started were all canned and his advice is not needed. He expresses his hope that Schmidt is enjoying retirement.

Schmidt leaves the building thinking he didn't have much of an impact and maybe that drunk at his retirement party was right. He goes home and buys an RV to drive around the country to discover what life is all about. Unfortunately, his plans are sidelined when his wife dies of a heart attack. Now what?

Meanwhile, Schmidt has started writing to an impoverished child in Africa and sending him money for food.

As the movie draws to a close, we see Schmidt's health begin to fail just as he receives a letter from the woman operating the mission in Africa. In her letter, she thanks him for the money he sent but, more importantly, she thanks him for his kind words to the boy. Enclosed with the letter is a painting from the boy as a token of his appreciation. Schmidt breaks down in tears, realizing he has finally made a difference. What a powerful message.

You see it's not about us. We are here to help others. It's not like that repulsive bumper sticker I saw on a minivan that said, "It's all about me." The owner of that vehicle just doesn't get it. I hope you do.

Here are a few tips to help you find happiness:

- It's not about you. In Israel, there are two bodies of water, the Sea of Galilee and the Dead Sea. Galilee has beautiful blue water, trees, fish, and an abundance of life. The Dead Sea has no life around it or in it. The difference is the Sea of Galilee has a river flowing in and a river flowing out. The Dead Sea has only a river flowing in. If you just take and do not give, your life is like the Dead Sea. Start the flow of giving and caring. You'll be much happier.

- Immediate gratification does not equal happiness. Discipline yourself not to go into debt for immediate gratification. Instead, invest for the future. The hope and peace of mind you will acquire if you live by this philosophy will bring contentment and a brighter, more comfortable future. Impulsive decisions are emotional decisions. Stick with logical decisions and delayed gratification.[4]

- Practice optimism. Think good thoughts. So much of our behavior and moods are affected by what's going on between our ears. As a bonus, it is well documented that optimists live longer than pessimists!

- Worry less. Worry and anxiety severely detract from the heartbeats slipping by. Worries shorten life over something that will soon pass or may never come to be. I remember a guy on his deathbed who said, "I wish I had not spent so much time worrying about things because 99 percent of the things I worried about never came to be."

Sir John Lubbock, in the 1800s, said, "A day of worry is more exhausting than a day of work."

A co-worker of mine, Adrian Allen is from Jamaica. He told me that when he came to America, he had to *learn* how to worry. What a statement about American vs. Jamaican philosophy.

- Expect less. How did Americans come to have such an overdeveloped sense of entitlement? You're much better off if you remember life is not fair. Expect less, so when you're blessed with more, how beautiful you will feel. I just feel lucky when I see all the fresh food in our markets. I traveled through forty-five countries throughout my career and saw some sad situations. Did you know that a Russian politician once took a tour of one of our grocery stores, and when he saw the water spray and heard the thunder sound effects in the produce section, he stormed out declaring, "Get me out of here! This is all staged."

- Give more. There are so many folks much worse off than you. It truly does feel better to give than to receive. One of the greatest gifts you can give is your time, and as I said before, that's what every hospice patient I have encountered wants—more time. Share more of that precious commodity with your family, friends, and neighbors. It's almost always easy to throw money at something, but not always so easy to devote more time to something.

- Practice altruism. Care about people more than yourself. Nothing makes me feel better than when

I have helped someone else out. I repeat, when you wrap up in yourself you make a pretty small package. You will never know your full potential and what you were put on this earth to do.

- Live simply. Daniel Boone said, "All a man needs to be happy is a good gun (for food), a good horse (for transportation), and a good wife (for companionship)."

We have managed to make things much more complicated as technology has advanced, but these are the basics.

One of my favorite places to be in my life was my "Grandma in Nebraska's" house in St. Paul, Nebraska. Her name was Opal Andersen. St. Paul, Nebraska is as close to Mayberry as any real town I've ever seen. My Grandpa, Bill Andersen, a first generation American, purchased the house in 1924. I don't believe it was any bigger than 900 square feet. It had two bedrooms, one where my dad and both his sisters were born, a family room, and an eat-in–kitchen—four rooms total. There was a hand-pump in the kitchen sink and an out-house out the back door. I remember sitting on the front porch and waving at neighbors, and relaxing on the old swing beneath a huge cottonwood tree. I felt peace and happiness there. I was at home; and boy was it simple.

Happiness

- Laugh more. In his book, *Making Life Rich Without Any Money*, Phil Callaway says the average toddler laughs two hundred times a day; the average adult only six times a day. Where have we lost 194 laughs? One guy approached me after hearing one of my talks and said, "Bills."

Yes, we have responsibilities, but there is still time to laugh...and it's better than Prozac! I've read that laughing lowers blood pressure, reduces stress, and improves blood chemicals.

I love Barney Fife from *The Andy Griffith Show* and Fred Sanford from *Sanford and Son*. Those guys crack me up, so I'll often sit down with my old DVDs for a good laugh.

- Maintain perspective; keep things in perspective. There will always be someone who is better off and someone who is worse off than you are. *Rich is a relative term.* Your doublewide looks pretty good to a homeless guy and your 1,500 square foot ranch looks pretty good to the homeless guy and the owner of the doublewide. Your 4,000 square foot home with the three-car garage looks great to all three of those previously mentioned; and a 6,500 square foot home on the ocean looks awesome to everyone, including the owner of the 4,000 square foot house. Need I go on?

A multi-billionaire was once asked how much money is enough. He said, "Just one more dollar." Where does it end?

I hope you see a common theme throughout this chapter on happiness. Expect less, value your relationships, be happy with what you have, and enjoy each day. Please care about others. You find true happiness by making a difference in the lives of others. I don't want to be your hospice volunteer and hear you express your regrets of time wasted in pursuing things that do not count. The day to start is now. Your birth certificate is your invitation to engage in life. You don't get a second chance.

I think one of the best descriptions of what life is all about and why we're here is in the recent movie *The Bucket List*. The line was delivered from the top of a pyramid in Egypt. You see, Jack Nicholson and Morgan Freeman's characters are dying of cancer, and as they contemplate death, they both learn much about what is really important.

I got so excited while watching the movie in the theater. And when I heard this quote, I actually had popcorn fly out of my mouth as I said to my wife, "That's it! The real key to life and happiness." Morgan Freeman and Jack Nicholson are sitting on top of one of the pyramids in Egypt and Freeman asks Nicholson, "Do you

Happiness

know what the Egyptians believe are the two questions you're asked before you go to heaven?"

"Did you have joy in your life and did your life give joy to anyone else?"

Morgan Freeman, The Bucket List

Living Well

My Happiness Checklist
(Things I will do to increase my joy)

1. _____

2. _____

3. _____

4. _____

5. _____

Chapter XVIII
Aging

When George Burns was ninety-five years old, he was asked, "What's good about being ninety-five?"

He answered simply, "Lack of peer pressure."

Most Americans have a fear of growing old. I guess we don't want our lives to end, and many fear the unknown. I believe, like the ugly caterpillar that blossoms into a beautiful butterfly, we too will morph into a magnificent heavenly spirit and wonder why we worried. Countless witnesses have gone to the other side and returned to report that it was wonderful, and they did not want to come back. Plus, my faith tells me it will be awesome.

America is one of the few countries on earth that does not overtly honor its elders. In many far eastern countries, the elderly are honored for their wisdom and experience. We are a "what's in it for me" society, which, again, speaks to our materialistic nature. The result is that we regard our elderly as burdens and a slow drain on our economy and time. Also, one of the reasons we have fewer kids now is that many people think that it is too expensive to have children. Many adults worry that they won't be able to have as many toys if they have children to support. They fear they will not have enough *things* that they think will make life better.

I was in a grocery store a few years ago and saw a woman who had to be at least seventy-five years old. She was wearing a leather mini-skirt and tons of makeup. It was not a pleasant site. Why do we try to mask who we are and refuse to be happy with that phase of our lives? Aging is simply part of the entire life process. When I first started to show a few gray hairs a couple of years back, one of my boys asked me, "Dad, are you going to dye your hair?"

"No I'm not," I replied. "I'm going to age gracefully and be happy with this stage of life." I think it shows incredible vanity to try to be something you're not… and it makes a statement about you. There is a great deal of strength in humility and being comfortable in your own skin, no matter how old it is!

As we age, let's enjoy the time we have left and honor those who are older. Let us take heed as they impart wisdom that is so desperately needed by the next generation. Even if this book had never been published, I knew somewhere this little manuscript would still exist for generations to come, as a few thoughts to pass on.

I would love to read something like this from my great-grandpa, who came to America from Denmark around 1875.

When I was a younger man, I would go in for my flight physicals and enjoy hearing the doctors rave about the strength of my eyes and my wonderful blood counts. Now I use "cheaters" to read, and all my blood tests are heading in a direction I do not want them to go. My memory is definitely slipping. I ache like my dad used to, and like I never thought I would. But I'm slowly learning to go with the flow (several times a night now). I even kind of chuckle about it and try to see the positive side of things. I told my wife the other day that there were some positives to my memory loss. For example, I'm always meeting new friends and I can hide my own Easter eggs now.

"When I was 40 my doctor advised me that a man in his forties shouldn't play tennis anymore. I carefully heeded his advice and couldn't wait till I turned 50 to start again."

Hugo Black, Supreme Court Justice

My Aging Checklist
(What will I do to enjoy and embrace the aging process?)

1. _____

2. _____

3. _____

4. _____

5. _____

Chapter XIX
Dying

A final end date and our funeral is something all of us will eventually have. Statistics show one out of one die. It could be this year, but most likely it's on a future calendar that has yet to be printed, but you never really know.

So how are you going to be remembered? What will people say about you when you are gone? Will there be anyone there to say anything?

I attended a funeral for a friend of mine who committed suicide a couple of years ago. He was special to me. I took him under my wing and gave him special training to get him through Navy instructor pilot training at VP-30.

He was having some family issues with the birth of a son and I knew he needed extra care. He was an airline pilot at the time he took his life. He left behind a beautiful wife and three children. As with most men's suicides, he may have felt he had lost his ability to provide for his family, and lost his sense of self worth.

I cannot over emphasize how important it is to instill that concept in everyone you meet in your life. Let them know you are glad they were born, because you never know where they are in this crazy, brief, stress-filled life.

His funeral was a tough one to get through because I watched eight people go up and talk about what a terrific guy he was. They spoke about his heart and his love for people. They spoke about everything from his role as a father and coach to his ability to be a good neighbor. I thought to myself, "Boy that is how I would like to be remembered someday."

I don't agree with choosing the date you exit the earth, but he certainly did a good job in his short life, and he cared deeply about others. I'm not sure we'll ever know what went wrong with his thinking, but while he was with us, he left some warm and caring footprints to follow.

I saw a couple of headstones on the Internet from, I believe, London, England. Who knows for sure? After all, I can barely find my car keys.

One of these headstones read, "She died for want of things." The one next to it read, "He died trying to give them to her." Nice legacy, huh? I think it might read better if it said, "She died trying to make everyone's life better."

Dying

I'm not sure if you've ever heard of the comedian, Stephen Wright. He has a very dry and subdued delivery that fits his beautiful manipulation of the English language. He has quite a following. He said once, "I finally figured out what to put on my tombstone. You're next."

I have been to quite a few funerals now and they are increasing in frequency as I age. I've lost my Naval Academy roommate to a car accident, my best civilian friend to a stroke, my VP-30 flying partner to a heart attack, and several friends to suicide. When I have come out of the church after such a service, I have never seen a U-Haul behind the hearse. You cannot take it with you.

Forgive me if you've heard this before, but I have heard this from numerous speakers and authors and enjoy it. So just in case you haven't, here it is: You did not have a choice as to what date was going to be on the left side of your tombstone. You didn't get to pick your parents or the country in which you were born, but I hope you're doing the best you can with the cards you were dealt. I hope and pray you do not pick the date you exit this life.

There is one thing you can and should control, however, and that is that little dash between those dates. How are you living your dash right now? When you are staring at death, as we all will, you can clearly see what was truly important and what should have been your focus. Again, heart and relationships matter most at the end of your journey. Make that dash mean something. You'll be so glad you did.

I often ask my audiences how many people can name the last five Super Bowl champions. A few folks usually can. Ok, how many can name the last five World Series champions? How many can name the last five Nobel Peace Prize winners or Miss Americas? These all are fairly famous people, but we can't remember their names. Now, how many of you can remember a friend, shipmate, neighbor, or teacher who really made a difference in your life? Each and every arm in the room goes up.

I don't care how successful you are or what your net worth is; those things are fleeting and will mean little in the end. What does matter is that each and every one of us has the ability to be that special person to someone and make a difference in his/her life. Your spouse, parents, kids, neighbors, co-workers, and friends need you.

I beg you all to be that special person to someone. There are people who desperately need your help out there and the picture is getting worse. Stress levels continue to rise with global terrorism and economic challenges.

I pray daily for those who have been devastated by our economic crisis, but also feel that this will produce a materialistic cleansing that we have needed for some time. People will discover that a roof over their head and any food on the table is a good thing. The size of the roof is not that important; it's how we make a difference to those folks who live under those rooftops. As America and the world emerge from this crisis—and we will—hopefully we'll have discovered the ingredients to true happiness as we approach eternity together.

"I urge you to live your life so that when you die even the undertaker will be sorry."

Mark Twain

My Funeral Checklist
(What things do I hope are said at my eulogy?)

1. _____

2. _____

3. _____

4. _____

5. _____

Chapter XX
Closing

Here I sit again on another airplane. This time a Northwest flight headed for a speech in Detroit to the number one Navy recruiting district in the United States. Someone who heard me speak asked me to share a few words with his command. I consider each one of these talks so important. I know I won't see most of these folks again in this life, and I know most in the room are either going through some crisis or headed for one eventually. Like I said before, we all have issues and you just never know how many generations deep your words may go. That is why I emphasize how important the words are that come out of your spirit and through your mouth. I try not to let anything out that will wound someone's spirit.

I want to leave you with three stories that kind of feed into each other and should leave you with the gist of a message that is counter to the way most of society thinks today.

Imagine a person walking down the beach on a hot, sunny, summer afternoon. He sees a starfish lying on the beach and knows it will eventually die from the heat, and dry up on the beach. So the man bends down and tosses it back into the ocean. He continues his walk and finds a few others that will soon perish and saves their lives. Another man, out for his daily jog, runs by, and asks the starfish rescuer what he is doing. He replies, "I'm throwing this starfish back in the ocean so it doesn't die."

The jogger says, "What difference does it make? There are literally thousands of them scattered on the beaches of the world."

Our strolling starfish rescuer responds by picking up a single starfish and commenting, "It makes a difference to this one," before tossing it back into the waves.

I know each one of you reading this book today has a few starfish in your circle of influence that are drying up on the beaches of life. I can just feel the names floating through your head. You know who they are—retracting from life due to some circumstance, be it divorce, poor health, money issues, or maybe just disenchantment about life. Maybe they are tired of trying to figure out what it's all about. You have the ability to let them know that they are important to someone...to you. People just need to know that they are loved and that their life has significance. It takes no money or athletic talent,

Closing

just a kind and caring heart. I implore you as your life continues to unfold to look for those starfish and make an emotional deposit with them. Help them find their way back into the ocean of life.

The next story is one I read on the Internet. It is the true story of a young high school boy in inner city New York. I can't remember his name but let's just say it was Kyle. He was headed home from school one Friday afternoon and had a stack of books with him.

Kyle was what some folks would classify as a nerdy kid, with thick glasses and all the other traits that made him the brunt of bullies' jokes and aggression. As he was walking along, a few local bullies knocked him to the ground, breaking his glasses and sending his books flying. He began to cry.

One of the high school football players, a linebacker named, let's say, Bill, saw what happened and came to Kyle's rescue. This kid, Bill, "got it" at a very young age. He dispersed the bullies and helped Kyle up. He helped collect his books and glasses and decided to take Kyle under his wing. Through the next few years, Bill taught Kyle how to lift weights and suggested he get contact lenses. He helped Kyle build some self-confidence.

As graduation for the pair approached, Kyle was valedictorian for their class and was to give the commencement address at graduation. Kyle began his address to the class by saying, "Today is not about me (another kid who got it at such a young age). It's about thanking

149

people who helped me get here. I want to thank my friend Bill, who a few years ago lent me a hand when I was down.

I had cleaned out my locker that day and I was headed home. I had the room picked out and my dad's loaded pistol hidden in it. I had planned to shoot myself through the mouth that night, but because of Bill's actions, I decided that life was worth living. Thank you my friend."

Kyle is now a doctor, saving people's lives in inner city New York. What difference do you think that one starfish made that day? Huge. You have them in your life and you have the ability to make a difference.

I finish with the story of Jackie Robinson. We all know he was the first black professional major league baseball player, but not many people know what he has written on his tombstone...but I'll get to that in a minute.

First, I want to tell you about the white man who played shortstop next to Jackie at second base. His name was Pee Wee Reese. One day, a petition was passed around the dugout that basically read, "We will not go out on the field with a black man." Pee Wee Reese tore the petition in two.

I also read that during a game in Cincinnati in 1947, Jackie was having a bad day. The crowd was riding him hard with racial taunts. He had just about had enough when Pee Wee Reese came off of shortstop, put his arm around Jackie in front of sixty thousand jeering spectators, and stared down some of the worst hecklers.

Closing

He was saying, in effect, this is my friend, a wonderful person, and a great ball player. To Robinson, he was saying, "Don't listen to these people. Just turn around and make it happen."

Jackie said that moment had a big impact on his life and he would never forget it.[1] Pee Wee Reese was truly a man with a wonderful heart and possessed the strength of character to do the right thing. Pee Wee Reese threw a starfish back into the ocean that day.

With all that Jackie accomplished in his brilliant career—the batting titles and championships—his tombstone in Cypress Hills Cemetery in Brooklyn, New York has one simple statement:

"A life is not important except in the impact it has on other lives."[2]

Thank you for your valuable time in reading this little book. I ask one small favor. With the decreasing heartbeats that you have left, use these little checklists, and go out there into this crazy world and look for those starfish. When you find them, throw them back into the sea of life…and *make a difference.*

God's peace to you all…Andy

Afterword

My first thought is to thank you again for taking your precious time to read my message in the face of the pace of life, which continues at break neck speed. I cannot possibly begin to change the mindset of America and this world without your help. I need you to have an effect on your circle of influence. The number of people that you will come in contact with during your lifetime is incredible.

I hope you get the gist of the message contained in this little book of checklists. If you don't get it now, maybe someday, as you age, you will—the sooner the better for you and all who know you. If we can change our materialistic mindset, begin to focus on relationships, and adopt a servant attitude (it's not about you), then happiness and a joy that never ends will manifest itself in your heart and soul.

You will make those around you happier, which in turn feeds back to you and becomes a self-fulfilling prophecy. It is not a difficult concept, but one that has been lost by so many. I am amazed by how many people are hungry for this message. We have to grab this momentum soon, before America collapses from within. Living this way is truly a win-win situation.

In working with Hospice all these years, again, I reiterate, these folks making the transition from life to death want to know that their lives had meaning. They want to know that they made a difference and left foot-prints that others will want to follow.

As I have described in the text, this power lies well within your capability. I have given you a few ideas and hopefully touched your heart. Your family, friends, and country need you now.